T0224973

SpringerBriefs in Computer Science

SpringerBriefs present concise summaries of cutting-edge research and practical applications across a wide spectrum of fields. Featuring compact volumes of 50 to 125 pages, the series covers a range of content from professional to academic.

Typical topics might include:

- A timely report of state-of-the art analytical techniques
- A bridge between new research results, as published in journal articles, and a contextual literature review
- A snapshot of a hot or emerging topic
- An in-depth case study or clinical example
- A presentation of core concepts that students must understand in order to make independent contributions

Briefs allow authors to present their ideas and readers to absorb them with minimal time investment. Briefs will be published as part of Springer's eBook collection, with millions of users worldwide. In addition, Briefs will be available for individual print and electronic purchase. Briefs are characterized by fast, global electronic dissemination, standard publishing contracts, easy-to-use manuscript preparation and formatting guidelines, and expedited production schedules. We aim for publication 8–12 weeks after acceptance. Both solicited and unsolicited manuscripts are considered for publication in this series.

**Indexing: This series is indexed in Scopus, Ei-Compendex, and zbMATH **

Yan Huang • Liang Wang

Deep Cognitive Networks

Enhance Deep Learning by Modeling Human
Cognitive Mechanism

 Springer

Yan Huang
Institute of Automation
Chinese Academy of Sciences
Beijing, China

Liang Wang
Institute of Automation
Chinese Academy of Sciences
Beijing, China

ISSN 2191-5768   ISSN 2191-5776   (electronic)
SpringerBriefs in Computer Science
ISBN 978-981-99-0278-1   ISBN 978-981-99-0279-8   (eBook)
https://doi.org/10.1007/978-981-99-0279-8

This Springer imprint is published by the registered company Springer Nature Singapore Pte Ltd.
The registered company address is: 152 Beach Road, #21-01/04 Gateway East, Singapore 189721, Singapore

Preface

Although deep learning models have achieved great progress recently, there still exists a large performance gap between deep learning models and the human cognitive system. Many researchers argue that one of the major reasons accounting for the performance gap is that deep learning models and the human cognitive system process external information in very different ways.

To mimic the performance gap, since 2014, there has been a trend to model various cognitive mechanisms in human brains, e.g., attention and memory, based on deep learning models. This book unifies these new kinds of deep learning models and calls them Deep Cognitive Networks (DCNs), which can implement various cognitive functions, e.g., selective extraction and knowledge reuse, for more effective information processing.

This book first collects existing theories and evidences about cognitive mechanism modeling from cognitive psychology and proposes a general framework of DCNs that jointly models multiple cognitive mechanisms. Then, it analyzes related works of DCNs and focuses primarily, but not exclusively, on the taxonomy of four key cognitive mechanisms (i.e., attention, memory, reasoning, and decision). At last, it summarizes the recent progress and discusses open problems and future trends.

We hope that this book provides a useful reference toward DCNs for researchers, practitioners, and students working on related areas.

Beijing, China   Yan Huang
December 2022

Acknowledgments

We express our deep gratitude to Yijun Guo and Qiyue Yin, who have helped us write this book. We would like to thank Lanlan Chang, Jingying Chen, and Sudha Ramachandran at Springer for their kind help and patience during the preparation of this book. We acknowledge the financial support by National Key Research and Development Program of China (2016YFB1001000), Key Research Program of Frontier Sciences CAS (ZDBS-LY-JSC032), and National Natural Science Foundation of China (61525306, 61633021, 61721004, 62236010, and 62276261).

Contents

Chapter 1
Introduction

Abstract This chapter provides an overview of the book. First, we introduce the background of Deep Cognitive Networks (DCNs), including their importance and brief history. Then, we analyze the motivation of DCNs and define their scope of modeling key cognitive mechanisms such as attention, memory, reasoning and decision. Finally, we outline the content organization of this book.

Keywords Deep learning · Deep cognitive networks

1.1 Background

Since 2006, deep learning [1–3] has achieved great success in basic perception tasks such as object recognition [4], machine translation [5] and speech recognition [6]. However, in more complex real-world scenarios, there still exists a huge performance gap between the state-of-the-art deep learning models and humans. In particular, although by performing supervised learning on large-scale datasets, current deep learning models [7–11] can only recognize one thousand predefined objects. While humans can easily recognize over ten thousands objects with much less supervised learning, and are much more robust to various factors of variation, e.g., illumination, view, resolution, etc. How to achieve human-level performance still remains to be a great challenge for deep learning models.

Recently, many researchers argue that one of major reasons accounting for the performance gap is: deep learning models and humans process the perceived information in very different ways. In particular, the deep learning models, e.g., Convolutional Neural Networks (CNNs) [12] and Recurrent Neural Networks (RNNs) [13], are originally proposed to simulate feedforward and recurrent connections among biological neurons in human brains. Although can effectively implement nonlinear mappings from input information to desired output such as class labels, they ignore to model the important cognitive mechanisms [14], which play essential roles during information processing in human brains. For example, visual attention [15, 16] is a very useful cognitive mechanism, which can

Y. Huang, L. Wang, *Deep Cognitive Networks*, SpringerBriefs in Computer Science,
https://doi.org/10.1007/978-981-99-0279-8_1

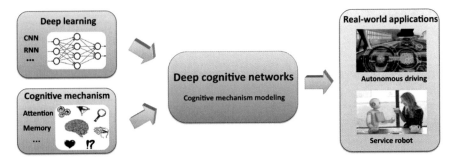

Fig. 1.1 The illustration of deep cognitive networks (DCNs)

selectively extract salient information to reduce the negative impact from redundant information in an image.

To alleviate this issue, there is a trend of modeling key cognitive mechanisms based on deep learning models, namely Deep Cognitive Networks (DCNs), as shown in Fig. 1.1. By implementing various cognitive abilities, e.g., selective information extraction, knowledge reuse and dynamic reasoning, DCNs can achieve much better performance than conventional deep learning models in many real-world applications. Since Weston et al. organized the first workshop of "Reasoning, Attention, Memory (RAM)",[1] attention-based DCNs [17–20] and memory-based DCNs [21–24] have been demonstrated to be very useful for so many tasks in computer vision and natural language processing. Later, reasoning-based DCNs [25–29] started to attract more attention, which are considered as a promising solution to achieving human-level performance of semantic reasoning and understanding.

In this book, we provide a comprehensive study of recent advances in DCNs. Considering that current most of existing DCNs model each cognitive mechanism individually, we first propose a general framework of DCNs that jointly models multiple mechanisms together like in human brains. The framework focuses primarily, but not exclusively on four key cognitive mechanisms[2] as follows.

1. **Attention**: it can concentrate on partial salient information while ignoring the redundant one. For example, a robot can selectively process object-related information in a scene, and reduce the negative impact from redundant background.
2. **Memory**: it can encode and store historical information to guide the processes of reasoning and decision. For example, even the object of otter appears only once in historical scenes, the robot can still remember its encoded information and later use it for recognition.

---

[1] http://www.thespermwhale.com/jaseweston/ram/.

[2] Note that we only consider four key cognitive mechanisms in the framework, since they are mostly considered and modeled in the current DCNs. In addition to them, more other cognitive mechanisms could also be incorporated into the framework in the future.

3. **Reasoning**: it can consciously solve problems by establishing the causal relation between premises and conclusions. For example, the robot can understand the relation among different objects in the scene, and infer their potential states.
4. **Decision**: it can select actions to interact with external environment by measuring possible outcomes. For example, after observing the current scene, the robot will choose to navigate to other scenes or stop here, to finally accomplish its goal.

In existing DCNs, their relation to important theories, computational models or experimental evidences in cognitive psychology [30, 31] is seldom discussed, which could limit the further development of DCNs. Thus, for each cognitive mechanism, we categorize related DCNs into representative classes and sub-classes, and analyze their relation to important theories, computational models and experimental evidences in cognitive psychology. At last, we discuss current open problems and outlook future trends.

1.2 Content Organization

The remaining chapters of this book are organized as follows:

- Chapter 2 illustrates a general framework of DCNs that includes representative principles for modeling different cognitive mechanisms. The principles mainly contain important theories, computational models and experimental evidences in cognitive psychology.
- Chapter 3 analyzes related works of attention-based DCNs and categories them into two classes including hard attention and soft attention. They are then further divided into five sub-classes including sequential attention, transformable attention, recurrent attention, channel attention and self attention.
- Chapter 4 analyzes related works of memory-based DCNs and categories them into two classes including short-term memory and long-term memory. They are then further divided into five sub-classes including working memory, short-term and long-term memory, episodic memory, conceptual memory and semantic memory.
- Chapter 5 analyzes related works of reasoning-based DCNs and categories them into two classes including analogical reasoning and deductive reasoning. They are then further divided into four sub-classes including memory reasoning, abstract reasoning, compositional reasoning and programmed reasoning.
- Chapter 6 analyzes related works of decision-based DCNs and categories them into two classes including normative decision and descriptive decision. They are then further divided into four sub-classes including sequential decision, group decision, emotional decision and imitative decision.
- Chapter 7 finally summarizes the properties and progress of current DCNs, and discusses current open problems and future trends from the perspectives of comprehensive modeling, model interpretability, evaluation scenario and computational cost.

References

1. Hinton, G.E., Salakhutdinov, R.R.: Reducing the dimensionality of data with neural networks. Science **313**(5786), 504–507 (2006)
2. Bengio, Y., Courville, A., Vincent, P.: Representation learning: a review and new perspectives. IEEE Trans. Pattern Anal. Mach. Intell. **35**(8), 1798–1828 (2013)
3. LeCun, Y., Bengio, Y., Hinton, G.: Deep learning. Nature **521**(7553), 436–444 (2015)
4. Krizhevsky, A., Sutskever, I., Hinton, G.E.: Imagenet classification with deep convolutional neural networks. In: Proceedings of the Advances in Neural Information Processing Systems, pp. 1097–1105 (2012)
5. Bahdanau, D., Cho, K., Bengio, Y.: Neural machine translation by jointly learning to align and translate. arXiv:1409.0473 (2014)
6. Graves, A., Mohamed, A.-R., Hinton, G.: Speech recognition with deep recurrent neural networks. In: Proceedings of the IEEE/CVF International Conference on Computer Vision, pp. 6645–6649. IEEE, Piscataway (2013)
7. Simonyan, K., Zisserman, A.: Very deep convolutional networks for large-scale image recognition. arXiv:1409.1556 (2014)
8. Russakovsky, O., Deng, J., Su, H., Krause, J., Satheesh, S., Ma, S., Huang, Z., Karpathy, A., Khosla, A., Bernstein, M., et al., Imagenet large scale visual recognition challenge. Int. J. Comput. Vis. **115**(3), 211–252 (2015)
9. He, K., Zhang, X., Ren, S., Sun, J.: Deep residual learning for image recognition. In: Proceedings of the IEEE Conference on Computer Vision and Pattern Recognition, pp. 770–778 (2016)
10. Ren, S., He, K., Girshick, R., Sun, J.: Faster R-CNN: towards real-time object detection with region proposal networks. In: Proceedings of the Advances in Neural Information Processing Systems, pp. 91–99 (2015)
11. Huang, G., Liu, Z., Van Der Maaten, L., Weinberger, K.Q.: Densely connected convolutional networks. In: Proceedings of the IEEE Conference on Computer Vision and Pattern Recognition, pp. 4700–4708 (2017)
12. LeCun, Y., Bottou, L., Bengio, Y., Haffner, P.: Gradient-based learning applied to document recognition. Proc. IEEE **86**(11), 2278–2324 (1998)
13. Schuster, M., Paliwal, K.K.: Bidirectional recurrent neural networks. IEEE Trans. Signal Process. **45**(11), 2673–2681 (1997)
14. Smith, E.E., Kosslyn, S.M.: Cognitive Psychology: Pearson New International Edition PDF eBook: Mind and Brain. Pearson Higher Education, New Jersey (2013)
15. Desimone, R., Duncan, J.: Neural mechanisms of selective visual attention. Ann. Rev. Neurosci. **18**(1), 193–222 (1995)
16. Olshausen, B.A., Anderson, C.H., Van Essen, D.C.: A neurobiological model of visual attention and invariant pattern recognition based on dynamic routing of information. J. Neurosci. **13**(11), 4700–4719 (1993)
17. Mnih, V., Heess, N., Graves, A., et al., Recurrent models of visual attention. Proc. Adv. Neural Inf. Process. Syst. **27** (2014)
18. Xu, K., Ba, J., Kiros, R., Cho, K., Courville, A., Salakhudinov, R., Zemel, R., Bengio, Y.: Show, attend and tell: neural image caption generation with visual attention. In: Proceedings of the International Conference on Machine Learning, pp. 2048–2057 (2015)
19. Jaderberg, M., Simonyan, K., Zisserman, A., et al., Spatial transformer networks. Proc. Adv. Neural Inf. Process. Syst. **28** (2015)
20. Vaswani, A., Shazeer, N., Parmar, N., Uszkoreit, J., Jones, L., Gomez, A.N., Kaiser, Ł., Polosukhin, I.: Attention is all you need. In: Proceedings of the Advances in Neural Information Processing Systems, vol. 30 (2017)
21. Weston, J., Chopra, S., Bordes, A.: Memory networks. arXiv:1410.3916 (2014)
22. Graves, A., Wayne, G., Danihelka, I.: Neural turing machines. arXiv:1410.5401 (2014)

23. Graves, A., Wayne, G., Reynolds, M., Harley, T., Danihelka, I., Grabska-Barwińska, A., Colmenarejo, S.G., Grefenstette, E., Ramalho, T., Agapiou, J., et al., Hybrid computing using a neural network with dynamic external memory. Nature **538**(7626), 471–476 (2016)

24. Sukhbaatar, S., Weston, J., Fergus, R., et al., End-to-end memory networks. Proc. Adv. Neural Inf. Process. Syst. **28** (2015)

25. Zheng, K., Zha, Z.-J., Wei, W.: Abstract reasoning with distracting features. In: Proceedings of the Advances in Neural Information Processing Systems, vol. 32 (2019)

26. Barrett, D., Hill, F., Santoro, A., Morcos, A., Lillicrap, T.: Measuring abstract reasoning in neural networks. In: Proceedings of the International Conference on Machine Learning. The Proceedings of Machine Learning Research, pp. 511–520 (2018)

27. Andreas, J., Rohrbach, M., Darrell, T., Klein, D.: Neural module networks. In: Proceedings of the IEEE Conference on Computer Vision and Pattern Recognition, pp. 39–48 (2016)

28. Neelakantan, A., Le, Q.V., Sutskever, I.: Neural programmer: Inducing latent programs with gradient descent. arXiv:1511.04834 (2015)

29. Johnson, J., Hariharan, B., Van Der Maaten, L., Hoffman, J., Fei-Fei, L., Lawrence Zitnick, C., Girshick, R.: Inferring and executing programs for visual reasoning. In: Proceedings of the IEEE International Conference on Computer Vision, pp. 2989–2998 (2017)

30. Gazzaniga, M.S., Ivry, R.B., Mangun, G.R.: Cognitive Neuroscience. The Biology of the Mind, 3rd edn. Norton & Company, New York (2009)

31. Anderson, J.R.: Cognitive Psychology and its Implications. Macmillan, London (2005)

Chapter 2
General Framework

Abstract This chapter describes a general framework of Deep Cognitive Networks (DCNs) in the context of an example task of vision language navigation. The framework elaborates major principles from the viewpoint of cognitive psychology, when jointly modeling multiple cognitive mechanisms in terms of attention, memory, reasoning and decision.

Keywords Deep cognitive networks · Cognitive psychology · Cognitive mechanism modeling

2.1 Overview

In the next, we attempt to propose a general framework of Deep Cognitive Networks (DCNs), which summarizes important principles when jointly modeling multiple cognitive mechanisms from the viewpoint of cognitive psychology. It could serve as the theoretical foundation for the following analysis and taxonomy of current DCNs, as well as the guidance for future model design. For the modeling of different cognitive mechanisms, we do not model them in isolation, but try to consider their cooperative relation in the context of the same vision language navigation task. As shown in Fig. 2.1, the task requires a robot to navigate to a scene to find an object by following a given linguistic instruction. During this procedure, various cognitive mechanisms will be activated and explained as follows.

2.2 Attention

When initializing the robot at a starting point and giving it an instruction: "go to the kitchen and find the table lamp", it will first perceive the current visual scene and represent it as an image. Since the content of image involves much redundant background information, it will activate the attention mechanism to selectively process salient image regions, and then evaluate whether it is the mentioned object

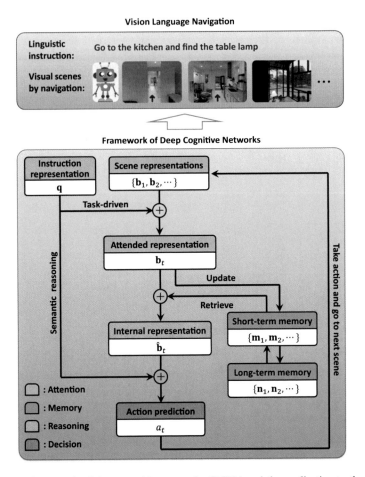

Fig. 2.1 The framework of deep cognitive networks (DCNs) and the application to the task of vision language navigation

like "table lamp". This might contain two sub-process: bottom-up attention and top-down attention [1]. The bottom-up attention is a data-driven process, which decides some regions in the image to be salient purely by the relation to their surroundings, for example based on the center-surround principle [2, 3]. In the figure, we use $\{\mathbf{b}_1, \mathbf{b}_2, \cdots\}$ to represent region representations in the image scene after the bottom-up attention. During this process, the Feature Integration Theory [4] can be modeled to integrate basic features (e.g., colors, shape or movement) to represent potential objects in different regions.

The top-down attention is a task-driven process, in which the given instruction is used as guidance to decide the attended representation $\mathbf{b}_t$. In the figure, we keep only salient region representations and completely neglect the rest in a "hard" manner, which is consistent with the Filter Theory [5] and Spotlight Theory [6].

Another feasible way is to degenerate rather than neglect the rest in a "soft" manner, which is similar to the Attenuation Theory [7]. In addition, the Biased Competition Theory [8] advocates that different objects compete for visual processing, and the processing can be biased toward to certain features of salient objects.

2.3 Memory

After obtaining the attended representation, the next step for the robot is to interact with its memory for information storage and reuse. According to how long the information is stored, there are mainly two types of memories: short-term memory [9] and long-term memory [10]. The short-term memory can only retain a limited amount of information encoded from attended representations at different timesteps, i.e., $\{\mathbf{m}_1, \mathbf{m}_2, \cdots\}$. The stored information can only last for a few seconds or minutes, because it will automatically decay [11] or be interfered by other information [12]. The stored information in the short-memory can be read out by serial search or exhaustive search [13] for later reuse. The short-term memory could be upgraded as working memory [14], which additionally allows for the manipulation of stored information for the following processes of reasoning and decision [15].

Short-term memory and long-term memory are closely related, since elaborative rehearsal can help move the stored information from short-term memory to long-term memory [16, 17], i.e., $\{\mathbf{n}_1, \mathbf{n}_2, \cdots\}$. Different from shot-term memory, long-term memory can store information for much longer time with a larger capacity. There are mainly episodic information and semantic information [18] in the long-term memory, which refer to past events and general world knowledge, respectively. These are also two types of explicit memory [19], in which stored information can be consciously recalled. The counterpart is implicit memory [20], in which stored information is used unconsciously but can affect thoughts and behaviours.

2.4 Reasoning

With the help of memories, the robot can combine the visual scene and linguistic instruction to reason the desired object. If the scene is previously unseen, it might perform analogical reasoning [21] by first retrieving similar information from the memories, and then using it to enhance the attended representation $\mathbf{b}_t$ to obtain the internal representation $\hat{\mathbf{b}}_t$. It is consistent with two important theories in cognitive psychology, i.e., the Structure Mapping Theory [22, 23] and Learning and Inference with Schemas and Analogies [24, 25]. They both regard the analogical reasoning as a structural mapping process from existing source information or knowledge in the memories to related target problem.

After that, deductive reasoning [26] might be activated, which is the process of obtaining a logical conclusion from one or more premises. In this case, the internal representation $\hat{\mathbf{b}}_t$ should ideally indicate the important scene information as the first premise: "this scene is bathroom and does not contain the table lamp". The instruction representation $\mathbf{q}$ indicates the second premise: "kitchen has the table lamp". Then the conclusion is: "go to other scenes and find the kitchen". To achieve this, a feasible way is to model the deductive reasoning as logical operations [27, 28].

2.5   Decision

As the robot cannot find the desired object in the current scene, it has to make decisions to take actions (e.g., left, right, forward and backward) to go to other scenes. In the figure, the predicted action at the current timestep is a_t. The decision making is a dynamic process, which involves multiple steps of interaction between the robot and environment. The decision making can be either rational or irrational, corresponding to normative decision or descriptive decision [29] in cognitive psychology, respectively. The normative decision defines how to rationally make good decisions to obtain maximum utility. The representative theories are Expected Utility Theory [30] and Multi-attribute Utility Theory [31], both of which choose an action that will result in the highest expected utility at each timestep.

While the descriptive decision focuses on how humans actually make decisions in practice, which does not guarantee the decisions to be good or rational. An important principle is satisfying [32], i.e., humans do not have to make the optimal decision every time, and a satisfying one is enough. Another principle is elimination by aspects [33], which can eliminate some alternatives by certain criteria, which can reduce the cognitive overload facing too much information [34]. In addition, emotion is an important factor interfering with rational decision making [35], which should also be considered and modeled.

2.6   Brief Summary

After the information processing by these cognitive mechanisms, the robot is likely to finally find the desired object. However, the proposed framework is still in its preliminary stage, which only contains four commonly modeled cognitive mechanisms. In human brains, there are more cognitive mechanisms participating in processing the external information. The whole procedure could be very complex, and even cognitive psychologists cannot fully explain all the details. Thus, more cognitive mechanisms could also be incorporated into the framework in the future.

In the next chapter, we will take the same order of illustrated cognitive mechanisms above to analyze related works in terms of attention-based DCNs, memory-based DCNs, reasoning-based DCNs and decision-based DCNs.

References

1. Connor, C.E., Egeth, H.E., Yantis, S.: Visual attention: bottom-up versus top-down. Curr. Biol. **14**(19), 850–852 (2004)
2. Carr, T.H., Dagenbach, D.: Semantic priming and repetition priming from masked words: evidence for a center-surround attentional mechanism in perceptual recognition. J. Exp. Psychol. Learn. Memory Cognit. **16**(2), 341 (1990)
3. Itti, L., Koch, C., Niebur, E.: A model of saliency-based visual attention for rapid scene analysis. IEEE Trans. Pattern Anal. Mach. Intell. **20**(11), 1254–1259 (1998)
4. Treisman, A.M., Gelade, G.: A feature-integration theory of attention. Cognit. Psychol. **12**(1), 97–136 (1980)
5. Broadbent, D.E.: The selective nature of learning. Percept. Commun. 244–267 (1958). https://psycnet.apa.org/record/2004-16224-010
6. Hoffman, J.E., Nelson, B.: Spatial selectivity in visual search. Percept. Psychophys. **30**(3), 283–290 (1981)
7. Treisman, A.M.: Contextual cues in selective listening. Quart. J. Exp. Psychol. **12**(4), 242–248 (1960)
8. Desimone, R., Duncan, J.: Neural mechanisms of selective visual attention. Annu. Rev. Neurosci. **18**(1), 193–222 (1995)
9. Miller, G.A.: The magical number seven, plus or minus two: some limits on our capacity for processing information. Psychol. Rev. **63**(2), 81 (1956)
10. Shiffrin, R.M., Atkinson, R.C.: Storage and retrieval processes in long-term memory. Psychol. Rev. **76**(2), 179 (1969)
11. Peterson, L., Peterson, M.J.: Short-term retention of individual verbal items. J. Exp. Psychol. **58**(3), 193 (1959)
12. Waugh, N.C., Norman, D.A.: The measure of interference in primary memory. J. Verbal Learn. Verbal Behavior **7**(3), 617–626 (1968)
13. Sternberg, S.: High-speed scanning in human memory. Science **153**(3736), 652–654 (1966)
14. Baddeley, A.D., Hitch, G.: Working memory. In: Psychology of Learning and Motivation, vol. 8, pp. 47–89. Elsevier, Amsterdam (1974)
15. Cowan, N.: What are the differences between long-term, short-term, and working memory? Progress Brain Res. **169**, 323–338 (2008)
16. Goldstein, E.B.: Cognitive Psychology: Connecting Mind, Research and Everyday Experience. Cengage Learning (2014)
17. Reisberg, D.: Cognition: Exploring the Science of the Mind. WW Norton & Company, New York (2010)
18. Tulving, E.: 12. Episodic and Semantic Memory. Organization of Memory/Eds E. Tulving, W. Donaldson. Academic Press, New York, pp. 381–403 (1972)
19. Squire, L.R.: Declarative and nondeclarative memory: multiple brain systems supporting learning and memory. J. Cognit. Neurosci. **4**(3), 232–243 (1992)
20. Schacter, D.L.: Implicit memory: history and current status. J. Exp. Psychol. Learn. Memory Cognit. **13**(3), 501 (1987)
21. Clement, C.A., Gentner, D.: Systematicity as a selection constraint in analogical mapping. Cognit. Sci. **15**(1), 89–132 (1991)
22. Falkenhainer, B., Forbus, K.D., Gentner, D.: The structure-mapping engine: algorithm and examples. Artif. Intell. **41**(1), 1–63 (1989)

23. Gentner, D.: Structure-mapping: a theoretical framework for analogy. Cognit. Sci. **7**(2), 155–170 (1983)
24. Hummel, J.E., Holyoak, K.J.: Distributed representations of structure: a theory of analogical access and mapping. Psychol. Rev. **104**(3), 427 (1997)
25. Hummel, J.E., Holyoak, K.J.: A symbolic-connectionist theory of relational inference and generalization. Psychol. Rev. **110**(2), 220 (2003)
26. Falmagne, R.J., Gonsalves, J.: Deductive inference. Annu. Rev. Psychol. **46**(1), 525–559 (1995)
27. Braine, M.D., O'Brien, D.P.: A theory of if: a lexical entry, reasoning program, and pragmatic principles. Psychol. Rev. **98**(2), 182 (1991)
28. Rips, L.J.: The Psychology of Proof: Deductive Reasoning in Human Thinking. MIT Press, Cambridge (1994)
29. Smith, E.E., Kosslyn, S.M.: Cognitive Psychology: Pearson New International Edition PDF eBook: Mind and Brain. Pearson, London (2013)
30. Schoemaker, P.J.: The expected utility model: its variants, purposes, evidence and limitations. J. Econ. Literature **20**, 529–563 (1982)
31. Dyer, J.S., Fishburn, P.C., Steuer, R.E., Wallenius, J., Zionts, S.: Multiple criteria decision making, multiattribute utility theory: the next ten years. Manag. Sci. **38**(5), 645–654 (1992)
32. Simon, H.A.: A behavioral model of rational choice. Quart. J. Econ. **69**(1), 99–118 (1955)
33. Tversky, A.: Elimination by aspects: a theory of choice. Psychol. Rev. **79**(4), 281 (1972)
34. Payne, J.W.: Task complexity and contingent processing in decision making: an information search and protocol analysis. Organ. Behav. Hum. Perform. **16**(2), 366–387 (1976)
35. De Sousa, R.: The rationality of emotions. Dial. Can. Philos. Rev. **18**(1), 41–63 (1979)

Chapter 3
Attention-Based DCNs

Abstract This chapter first provides a brief overview of attention-based Deep Cognitive Networks (DCNs). Then, representative models from two aspects in terms of hard attention and soft attention are introduced and analyzed, as well as their relation to important theories, computational models and experimental evidences in cognitive psychology. At last, this chapter is briefly summarized.

Keywords Attention modeling · Soft attention · Self attention

3.1 Overview

Before the rise of deep learning, there were already a number of works [1] modeling the attention mechanism, namely visual saliency prediction. They usually take an image or a video as input and predict corresponding saliency maps, which indicate probabilities of being attended by human eyes. Since 2014, researchers have started to use the technique of deep learning and proposed various attention-based DCNs [2–4], which have diverse applications in computer vision, natural language processing and data mining. As shown in Table 3.1, we mainly focus on two classes of attention-based DCNs: hard attention and soft attention, and their six sub-classes: sequential attention, transformable attention, recurrent attention, cross-modal attention, channel attention and self attention. The representative attention-based DCNs include Sequential Attention Model [2], Spatial Transformer Network [5], Attention-based RNN [3], Hierarchical Question-image Co-attention [6], Squeeze-and-Excitation Network [7] and Transformer [8]. We also elaborate their related important theories, computational models and experimental evidences in cognitive psychology. The corresponding details will be explained in the following.

Table 3.1 The taxonomy of attention-based DCNs

Class	Sub-class	Representative DCN	Theory, model and evidence
Hard attention	Sequential attention	Sequential attention model [2], third-order Boltzmann machine [9]	Filter theory [10], spotlight theory [11], shifter circuits model [12]
	Transformable attention	Spatial transformer network [5], deep recurrent attentive writer [13]	
Soft attention	Recurrent attention	Attention-based RNN [3], show, attend and tell model [4]	Attenuation theory [14], cross-channel priming effect [15], feature integration theory [16], biased competition theory [17]
	Cross-modal attention	Hierarchical question-image co-attention [6]	
	Channel attention	Squeeze-and-excitation network [7]	
	Self attention	transformer [8]	

3.2   Hard Attention

In cognitive psychology, the Filter Theory [10] argues that visual information is filtered at the early stage during processing. The filter only selects salient information based on basic features such as color and direction. The Spotlight Theory [11] compares the focus of attention to a spotlight, in which the information outside of the spotlight is not received. Both them consider the attention in a "hard" manner, i.e., only focusing on salient or foreground information while completely ignoring the background information. Consistent with this, a series of hard attention models were proposed, which can be categorized into two sub-classes including sequential attention and transformable attention.

3.2.1   Sequential Attention

Sequential attention models consider the attention mechanism as a dynamic process that has multiple timesteps. At each timestep, the models are able to predict a location (e.g., spatial position in an image) that will be attended to in the next timestep (e.g., cropping the corresponding image region while ignoring the rest). To our knowledge, Larochelle and Hinton [9] proposed the first model of sequential attention based on a Third-order Boltzmann Machine, which can learn to recognize objects by combining observations at several timesteps. In the meantime, Denil et al. [18] proposed another model based on a factored Restricted Boltzmann Machine,

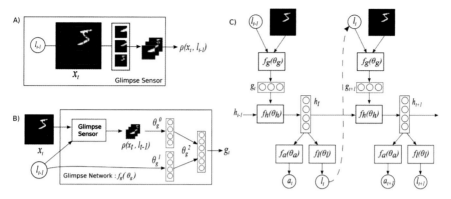

Fig. 3.1 Illustration of sequential attention model (SAM). (**a**) Given a location and an input image, the sensor extracts a region representation. (**b**) The extracted representation and location are mapped into a hidden space using linear layers to produce a glimpse representation. (**c**) Overall, the model is based on a RNN, which takes the glimpse representation as input, combines with the hidden state at previous timestep, and produces the new hidden state. The location network $f_l(\cdot)$ and action network $f_a(\cdot)$ use the hidden state to produce the next location. Figure is from [2]

which designs two interacting pathways, i.e., an identity one and a control one, to simulate the what and where pathways in human brains.

Later, as shown in Fig. 3.1, Mnih et al. [2] proposed the most representative model namely Sequential Attention Model (SAM). It is based on a RNN and Reinforcement Learning (RL) [19], which can selectively extract and process a fixed number of regions from an image. It formulates the attention as a Markov Decision Process (MDP), in which the action is defined as attended location prediction, the state is represented by the initial image or cropped image region, and the reward is maximized when an object is accurately recognized. Li et al. [20] extended the SAM by adding an extra binary action at every timestep, which learns to automatically decide when to stop the attention. Training RL-based models with only class label supervision is difficult, which makes them hard to scale to complex datasets. To deal with the problem, Elsayed et al. [21] performed a pretraining step, which is able to provide good initial attention locations for RL.

Up to now, the sequential attention models have been widely used in diverse applications especially in computer vision. In particular, similar ideas have been first proven to be useful for extracting informative regions in images, and achieved well performance in the tasks of object detection [22] and multi-label learning [23]. Then, other models have also been used to select representative frames in video analysis tasks such as action detection [24] and video face recognition [25].

There is also another kind of sequential attention model, which first uses CNNs to generate bounding boxes of objects, and then uses them as attended regions in a cascaded manner. Xiao et al. [26] designed both object-level attention and part-level attention based on CNNs in a classification way, which can selectively extract discriminative region representations from bounding boxes for the task of fine-grained recognition. In parallel, Gonzalez-Garcia et al. [27] proposed an active search strategy based on random forest and CNNs, which can select a sequence of bounding boxes from pre-obtained ones to improve the efficiency for the task of object detection. In addition to the boxes, some works rely on existing object segmentation models to generate object masks, and then use them to guide the attention process for the tasks of person re-identification [28] and salient object detection [29].

3.2.2 Transformable Attention

In cognitive psychology, Anderson and Van Essen [12] proposed the Shifter Circuits Model, which relatively aligns input arrays to output arrays with dynamic shifts, while preserving their respective spatial relation. It is later extended by Olshausen et al. [30] to obtain more position-invariant and scale-invariant representations of objects. Similar to them, Tang et al. [31] made an early attempt and proposed a transformable attention model, which uses 2D similarity transformations based on a Deep Belief Network (DBN) [32] to implement scaling, rotation and shift operations for the alignment. Most of the following transformable attention models similarly model the 2D form of transformable attention, where either an array of 2D Gaussian filters or a group of affine transformations is applied to the input image, producing a transformed image region that indicates the attended location.

As shown in Fig. 3.2, one of the most successful models in this direction is Spatial Transformer Network (STN) [5]. It first defines parameterized affine transformations including scaling, cropping, rotation and non-rigid deformations, and then performs them on the entire input feature map to obtain the output (attended) feature map. The model is flexible that can be incorporated into standard deep learning models to extract position-invariant and scale-invariant representations. Later, Sønderby et al. [33] combined the STN with a RNN as a recurrent STN, which is able to sequentially attend to multiple objects in an image. Lohit et al.

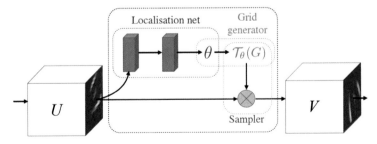

Fig. 3.2 Illustration of spatial transformer network (STN). The localisation network regresses the transformation parameters θ, which are then used by the grid generator to perform sampling in the input feature map to obtained the output feature map. Figure is from [5]

[34] proposed a temporal extension of STN to learn invariant and discriminative time warping, which show performance improvements in the task of 3D action recognition. Kim et al. [35] proposed a spatio-temporal transformer network for the task of video restoration. The model can estimate optical flow in both space and time, and then selectively warp target frames. Haque et al. [36] extended the STN from 2D to 3D space, which is able to improve the performance of 3D human pose estimation. In addition to these works, STN has also been demonstrated to be effective in other tasks such as person re-identification [37] and human gaze estimation [38].

Different from the affine transformations in STN, Gregor et al. [13] proposed a probabilistic model named Deep Recurrent Attentive Writer (DRAW). It alternatively uses an array of 2D Gaussian filters to smoothly generate image regions of varying locations and scales, indicating attended locations. Transformable attention has been successfully applied to the task of and instance segmentation [39].

3.3 Soft Attention

The major difference between soft attention and hard attention is that: when attending to an image, the hard attention completely ignores the redundant background information, while the soft attention chooses to exponentially suppress it and let it still have the chance to be processed. The main idea of soft attention is consistent with the Attenuation Theory [14], which can be regarded as an extended version of Filter Theory, since the unattended information is not completely blocked but just decreased. Similar to them, various soft attention models have been proposed and applied to many tasks in computer vision, natural language processing, speech processing and multimedia data analysis. Next, we will introduce four sub-classes of soft attention including recurrent attention, cross-modal attention, channel attention and self attention.

3.3.1 Recurrent Attention

Similar to the sequential attention, recurrent attention is also modeled as a dynamic process that has multiple timesteps. But the major difference is that the recurrent attention predicts attention weights for all candidate locations at each timestep, and uses them to adaptively aggregate representations of all locations. To our knowledge, Bahdanau et al. [3] proposed the first model of recurrent attention for the task of machine translation. At each timestep, the model first predicts attention weights for all candidate words in a source sentence based on Multi-Layer Perceptrons (MLPs), and then aggregates them to predict a word of target sentence in a weighted sum manner. The model can recurrently perform the attention multiple times to generate all desired words. Xu et al. [4] extended the idea for image

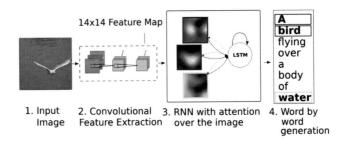

1. Input   2. Convolutional   3. RNN with attention   4. Word by
Image   Feature Extraction   over the image   word
                                                               generation

Fig. 3.3 Illustration of show, attend and tell (SAT) model for the task of image captioning. It includes four steps to generate a descriptive sentence from an input image. Figure is from [4]

captioning and proposed the Show, Attend and Tell (SAT) model, which can predict a 2D attention map for an image. As shown in Fig. 3.3, the attention map indicates the importance of all image regions and is used to guide the aggregation of region representations.

The recurrent attention might be the most widely used attention in computer vision. First, it can be directly applied to most image-based tasks including fine-grained recognition [40] and object detection [41], to attend to informative regions for performance improvements. Second, it can also be easily extended as temporal and spatio-temporal versions to select salient frames in video analysis tasks including captioning [42] and action recognition [43]. In addition, different from purely performing the attention on the input data, some other works implement the attention in a semantic-guided manner. In their models, the attention weights are computed based on the semantic information predicted from data such as attributes [44], words [45] or facts [46].

3.3.2   Cross-Modal Attention

In cognitive neuroscience, Driver et al. [47] and Kennett et al. [15] experimentally demonstrated the cross-channel priming effect in human brain. The effect refers to that one stimuli is able to facilitate the processing of other stimulus. Similar to this, Lu et al. [6] proposed a model named Hierarchical Question-image Co-attention (HQC), which includes two versions of cross-modal attention for the task of visual question answering.

As shown in Fig. 3.4a, b, to combine question (word-level) representations and image (region-level) representations to predict correct answers, the two versions of cross-modal attention both have to first compute a similarity matrix between two sets of representations, and then normalize it in either row (or column) axis as question-guided (or image-guided) attention weights to aggregate original representations. The major different between these two versions is that the parallel one performs the question-guided and image-guided attention simultaneously, while the alternative

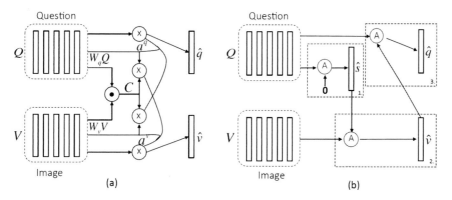

Fig. 3.4 Illustration of hierarchical question-image co-attention (HQC) for the task of visual question answering, which contains two versions of cross-modal attention: (**a**) a parallel one and (**b**) an alternating one. Figure is from [6]

one performs them in an alternative manner. Compared with a limited number of works [48] based on the alternative version, the parallel version has been studied more widely and applied to more tasks such as textual entailment [49] and image-text matching [50].

There is also another parallel version of cross-modal attention, which does not compute the similarity matrix to obtain attention weights. Instead, it uses deep learning models to predict modality-related attention weights directly from multimodal data. In this direction, Huang et al. [51] made an early attempt and successfully applied their models to the task of image-text matching. Similar ideas have also been explored in multi-object tracking [52] and video object segmentation [53].

3.3.3 Channel Attention

In a CNN, each convolutional layer takes multi-channel feature maps (or three-channel RGB images) as input and outputs its processed multi-channel feature maps. Each output feature map usually captures a certain kind of discriminative feature (e.g., color, edge and shape) that can be used for image classification or object detection. In 1980, Treisman and Gelade [16] proposed the Feature Integration Theory, which similarly argues that each kind of feature (e.g., color, edge and shape) is stored in a separated map, and all of them will be selectively integrated when looking for an object having multiple kinds of features. To our knowledge, Chen et al. [54] and Wang et al. [55] proposed two early versions of channel attention based on CNNs, which are closely related to the Feature Integration Theory. For each convolutional layer, the channel attention can assign different weights to different channels of input feature maps, and then accordingly aggregate them together.

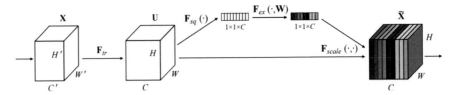

Fig. 3.5 Illustration of squeeze-and-excitation network (SENet). X and U are input multi-channel feature maps and their transformed version, respectively, $F_{ex}(\cdot, W)$ is the mapping to obtain channel-wise attention weights, and $\tilde{X}$ is the attended feature maps. Figure is from [7]

As shown in Fig. 3.5, the most influential model of channel attention is Squeeze-and-Excitation Network (SENet) [7], which is based on residual networks [56]. It demonstrated its effectiveness for image classification by winning the first place of the ImageNet Large Scale Visual Recognition Challenge (ILSVRC) in 2017 [57]. Later, various extensions of SENet were proposed from the perspectives of context aggregation [58], position modeling [59], scale invariance [60], and high-order statistics [61]. Up to now, the channel attention has been successfully applied to many tasks such as image super-resolution [62], frame interpolation [63] and scene segmentation [64].

3.3.4 Self Attention

Desimone and Duncan [17] proposed the well-known Biased Competition Theory, which views the process of attention as a competition among input features at different locations. The competition is usually biased toward certain features of an object that is currently attended to. Consistent with this, Vaswani et al. [8] proposed the first version of self attention, namely Scaled Dot-Product Attention (SDPA), which explicitly simulates such a competition[1] by first measuring inter-feature similarities and then using them to weight the input features, as shown in Fig. 3.6. Later, many extensions were proposed from the perspectives of position modeling [65], complexity reduction [66], and non-local filtering [67]. These models have been widely used in many applications such as speech recognition [68], image generation [69], semantic segmentation [70], point cloud generation [71], and traffic prediction [72].

---

[1] Although other forms of soft attention also somewhat impose the competition on the input features by the softmax function, they are more like normalization operations since each input feature is processed independently of the others.

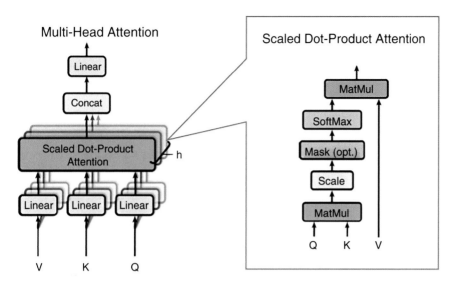

Fig. 3.6 Illustration of scaled dot-product attention (SDPA). It transforms input features into three versions: Q, K and V. The first two are compared to compute the similarities among input features, which are then used as attention weights to combine the V. Figure is from [8]

By combining the self attention and encoder-decoder architecture together, a new architecture namely Transformer [8] was proposed, as shown in Fig. 3.7. This model is widely studied and extended into different versions for diverse tasks, including Bidirectional Encoder Representations from Transformer (BERT) [73] for natural language processing, Vision Transformer (ViT) [74] for computer vision, Contrastive Language-Image Pre-Training (CLIP) [75] for multimodal learning, etc. Most of these models show three common properties: (1) they usually have to be pretrained on large-scale datasets via both supervised learning and self-supervised learning, (2) they usually have a large number of learning parameters that lower the model efficiency, and (3) they achieve the state-of-the-art performance on so many tasks and show strong generalization ability.

3.4 Brief Summary

Since 2014, a very large number of attention-based DCNs have been proposed. Due to the space limitation here, this chapter can only introduce partial representative works and might not cover very recent ones. These attention-based DCNs have studied the modeling of attention from various aspects in terms of background modeling, dynamical processing and channel aggregation. The effectiveness of these models have been extensively demonstrated in a wide range of applications in computer vision, natural language processing and multimodal data analysis.

Fig. 3.7 Illustration of
transformer. The overall
architecture contains the
encoder and decoder using
stacked self attention and
fully connected layers. Figure
is from [8]

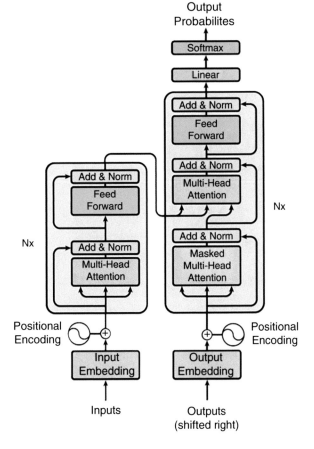

References

1. Borji, A., Itti, L.: State-of-the-art in visual attention modeling. IEEE Trans. Pattern Anal. Mach. Intell. **35**(1), 185–207 (2012)
2. Mnih, V., Heess, N., Graves, A., et al.: Recurrent models of visual attention. In: Proceedings of the Advances in Neural Information Processing Systems, vol. 27 (2014)
3. Bahdanau, D., Cho, K., Bengio, Y.: Neural machine translation by jointly learning to align and translate. arXiv:1409.0473 (2014)
4. Xu, K., Ba, J., Kiros, R., Cho, K., Courville, A., Salakhudinov, R., Zemel, R., Bengio, Y.: Show, attend and tell: neural image caption generation with visual attention. In: Proceedings of the International Conference on Machine Learning. The Proceedings of Machine Learning Research, pp. 2048–2057 (2015)
5. Jaderberg, M., Simonyan, K., Zisserman, A., et al.: Spatial transformer networks. In: Advances in Neural Information Processing Systems (2015)
6. Lu, J., Yang, J., Batra, D., Parikh, D.: Answering. In: Proceedings of the Advances in Neural Information Processing Systems, vol. 29 (2016)
7. Hu, J., Shen, L., Sun, G.: Squeeze-and-excitation networks. In: Proceedings of the IEEE Conference on Computer Vision and Pattern Recognition, pp. 7132–7141 (2018)

8. Vaswani, A., Shazeer, N., Parmar, N., Uszkoreit, J., Jones, L., Gomez, A.N., Kaiser, Ł., Polosukhin, I.: Attention is all you need. In: Proceedings of the Advances in Neural Information Processing Systems, vol. 30 (2017)

9. Larochelle, H., Hinton, G.E.: Learning to combine foveal glimpses with a third-order Boltzmann machine. In: Advances in Neural Information Processing Systems, vol. 23 (2010)

10. Lachter, J., Forster, K.I., Ruthruff, E.: Forty-five years after broadbent (1958): still no identification without attention. Psychol. Rev. **111**(4), 880 (2004)

11. Hoffman, J.E., Nelson, B.: Spatial selectivity in visual search. Percept. Psychophys. **30**(3), 283–290 (1981)

12. Anderson, C.H., Van Essen, D.C.: Shifter circuits: a computational strategy for dynamic aspects of visual processing. Proc. Natl. Acad. Sci. **84**(17), 6297–6301 (1987)

13. Gregor, K., Danihelka, I., Graves, A., Rezende, D., Wierstra, D.: Draw: a recurrent neural network for image generation. In: Proceedings of the International Conference on Machine Learning. The Proceedings of Machine Learning Research, pp. 1462–1471 (2015)

14. Treisman, A.M.: Contextual cues in selective listening. Quart. J. Exp. Psychol. **12**(4), 242–248 (1960)

15. Kennett, S., Spence, C., Driver, J.: Visuo-tactile links in covert exogenous spatial attention remap across changes in unseen hand posture. Percept. Psychophys. **64**(7), 1083–1094 (2002)

16. Treisman, A.M., Gelade, G.: A feature-integration theory of attention. Cognit. Psychol. **12**(1), 97–136 (1980)

17. Desimone, R., Duncan, J.: Neural mechanisms of selective visual attention. Annu. Rev. Neurosci. **18**(1), 193–222 (1995)

18. Denil, M., Bazzani, L., Larochelle, H., de Freitas, N.: Learning where to attend with deep architectures for image tracking. Neural Comput. **24**(8), 2151–2184 (2012)

19. Sutton, R. S., Barto, A.G., et al.: Introduction to reinforcement learning, vol. 135. MIT press, Cambridge (1998)

20. Li, Z., Yang, Y., Liu, X., Zhou, F., Wen, S., Xu, W.: Dynamic computational time for visual attention. In: Proceedings of the IEEE International Conference on Computer Vision Workshops, pp. 1199–1209 (2017)

21. Elsayed, G., Kornblith, S., Le, Q.V.: Saccader: improving accuracy of hard attention models for vision. In: Advances in Neural Information Processing Systems, vol. 32 (2019)

22. Caicedo, J.C., Lazebnik, S.: Active object localization with deep reinforcement learning. In: Proceedings of the IEEE International Conference on Computer Vision, pp. 2488–2496 (2015)

23. Ba, J., Mnih, V., Kavukcuoglu, K.: Multiple object recognition with visual attention. arXiv:1412.7755 (2014)

24. Yeung, S., Russakovsky, O., Mori, G., Fei-Fei, L.: End-to-end learning of action detection from frame glimpses in videos. In: Proceedings of the IEEE Conference on Computer Vision and Pattern Recognition, pp. 2678–2687 (2016)

25. Rao, Y., Lu, J., Zhou, J.: Attention-aware deep reinforcement learning for video face recognition. In: Proceedings of the IEEE International Conference on Computer Vision, pp. 3931–3940 (2017)

26. Xiao, T., Xu, Y., Yang, K., Zhang, J., Peng, Y., Zhang, Z.: The application of two-level attention models in deep convolutional neural network for fine-grained image classification. In: Proceedings of the IEEE Conference on Computer Vision and Pattern Recognition, pp. 842–850 (2015)

27. Gonzalez-Garcia, A., Vezhnevets, A., Ferrari, V.: An active search strategy for efficient object class detection. In: Proceedings of the IEEE Conference on Computer Vision and Pattern Recognition, pp. 3022–3031 (2015)

28. Song, C., Huang, Y., Ouyang, W., Wang, L.: Mask-guided contrastive attention model for person re-identification. In: Proceedings of the IEEE Conference on Computer Vision and Pattern Recognition, pp. 1179–1188 (2018)

29. Chen, S., Tan, X., Wang, B., Hu, X.: Reverse attention for salient object detection. In: Proceedings of the European Conference on Computer Vision, pp. 234–250 (2018)

30. Olshausen, B.A., Anderson, C.H., Van Essen, D.C.: A neurobiological model of visual attention and invariant pattern recognition based on dynamic routing of information. J. Neurosci. **13**(11), 4700–4719 (1993)
31. Tang, C., Srivastava, N., Salakhutdinov, R.R.: Learning generative models with visual attention. In: Proceedings of the Advances in Neural Information Processing Systems, vol. 27 (2014)
32. Hinton, G.E., Osindero, S., Teh, Y.-W.: A fast learning algorithm for deep belief nets. Neural Comput. **18**(7), 1527–1554 (2006)
33. Sønderby, S.K., Sønderby, C.K., Maaløe, L., Winther, O.: Recurrent spatial transformer networks. arXiv:1509.05329 (2015)
34. Lohit, S., Wang, Q., Turaga, P.: Temporal transformer networks: joint learning of invariant and discriminative time warping. In: Proceedings of the IEEE/CVF Conference on Computer Vision and Pattern Recognition, pp. 12426–12435 (2019)
35. Kim, T.H., Sajjadi, M.S., Hirsch, M., Scholkopf, B.: Spatio-temporal transformer network for video restoration. In: Proceedings of the European Conference on Computer Vision, pp. 106–122 (2018)
36. Haque, A., Peng, B., Luo, Z., Alahi, A., Yeung, S., Fei-Fei, L.: Towards viewpoint invariant 3d human pose estimation. In: Proceedings of the European Conference on Computer Vision, pp. 160–177. Springer, Berlin (2016)
37. Li, D., Chen, X., Zhang, Z., Huang, K.: Learning deep context-aware features over body and latent parts for person re-identification. In: Proceedings of the IEEE Conference on Computer Vision and Pattern Recognition, pp. 384–393 (2017)
38. Recasens, A., Kellnhofer, P., Stent, S., Matusik, W., Torralba, A.: Learning to zoom: a saliency-based sampling layer for neural networks. In: Proceedings of the European Conference on Computer Vision, pp. 51–66 (2018)
39. Ren, M., Zemel, R.S.: End-to-end instance segmentation with recurrent attention. In: Proceedings of the IEEE Conference on Computer Vision and Pattern Recognition, pp. 6656–6664 (2017)
40. Zhao, B., Wu, X., Feng, J., Peng, Q., Yan, S.: Diversified visual attention networks for fine-grained object classification. IEEE Trans. Multimedia **19**(6), 1245–1256 (2017)
41. Li, J., Wei, Y., Liang, X., Dong, J., Xu, T., Feng, J., Yan, S.: Attentive contexts for object detection. IEEE Trans. Multimedia **19**(5), 944–954 (2016)
42. Yao, L., Torabi, A., Cho, K., Ballas, N., Pal, C., Larochelle, H., Courville, A.: Describing videos by exploiting temporal structure. In: Proceedings of the IEEE International Conference on Computer Vision, pp. 4507–4515 (2015)
43. Sharma, S., Kiros, R., Salakhutdinov, R.: Action recognition using visual attention. arXiv:1511.04119 (2015)
44. You, Q., Jin, H., Wang, Z., Fang, C., Luo, J.: Image captioning with semantic attention. In: Proceedings of the IEEE Conference on Computer Vision and Pattern Recognition, pp. 4651–4659 (2016)
45. Yu, L., Lin, Z., Shen, X., Yang, J., Lu, X., Bansal, M., Berg, T.L.: Mattnet: modular attention network for referring expression comprehension. In: Proceedings of the IEEE Conference on Computer Vision and Pattern Recognition, pp. 1307–1315 (2018)
46. Lu, P., Ji, L., Zhang, W., Duan, N., Zhou, M., Wang, J.: R-VQA: learning visual relation facts with semantic attention for visual question answering. In: Proceedings of the ACM SIGKDD International Conference on Knowledge Discovery & Data Mining, pp. 1880–1889 (2018)
47. Driver, J., Spence, C.: Crossmodal attention. Curr. Opin. Neurobiol. **8**(2), 245–253 (1998)
48. Tan, H., Bansal, M.: LXMERT: learning cross-modality encoder representations from transformers. arXiv:1908.07490 (2019)
49. Yin, W., Schütze, H., Xiang, B., Zhou, B.: ABCNN: attention-based convolutional neural network for modeling sentence pairs. Trans. Assoc. Comput. Linguist. **4**, 259–272 (2016)
50. Lee, K.-H., Chen, X., Hua, G., Hu, H., He, X.: Stacked cross attention for image-text matching. In: Proceedings of the European Conference on Computer Vision, pp. 201–216 (2018)

51. Huang, Y., Wang, W., Wang, L.: Instance-aware image and sentence matching with selective multimodal LSTM. In: Proceedings of the IEEE Conference on Computer Vision and Pattern Recognition, pp. 2310–2318 (2017)
52. Zhu, J., Yang, H., Liu, N., Kim, M., Zhang, W., Yang, M.-H.: Online multi-object tracking with dual matching attention networks. In: Proceedings of the European Conference on Computer Vision, pp. 366–382 (2018)
53. Lu, X., Wang, W., Ma, C., Shen, J., Shao, L., Porikli, F.: See more, know more: unsupervised video object segmentation with co-attention siamese networks. In: Proceedings of the IEEE/CVF Conference on Computer Vision and Pattern Recognition, pp. 3623–3632 (2019)
54. Chen, L., Zhang, H., Xiao, J., Nie, L., Shao, J., Liu, W., Chua, T.-S.: SCA-CNN: Spatial and channel-wise attention in convolutional networks for image captioning. In: Proceedings of the IEEE Conference on Computer Vision and Pattern Recognition, pp. 5659–5667 (2017)
55. Wang, F., Jiang, M., Qian, C., Yang, S., Li, C., Zhang, H., Wang, X., Tang, X.: Residual attention network for image classification. In: Proceedings of the IEEE Conference on Computer Vision and Pattern Recognition, pp. 3156–3164 (2017)
56. He, K., Zhang, X., Ren, S., Sun, J.: Deep residual learning for image recognition. In: Proceedings of the IEEE Conference on Computer Vision and Pattern Recognition, pp. 770–778 (2016)
57. Russakovsky, O., Deng, J., Su, H., Krause, J., Satheesh, S., Ma, S., Huang, Z., Karpathy, A., Khosla, A., Bernstein, M., et al.: Imagenet large scale visual recognition challenge. Int. J. Comput. Vis. **115**(3), 211–252 (2015)
58. Li, X., Wu, J., Lin, Z., Liu, H., Zha, H.: Recurrent squeeze-and-excitation context aggregation net for single image deraining. In: Proceedings of the European Conference on Computer Vision, pp. 254–269 (2018)
59. Hou, Q., Zhou, D., Feng, J.: Coordinate attention for efficient mobile network design. In: Proceedings of the IEEE/CVF Conference on Computer Vision and Pattern Recognition, pp. 13713–13722 (2021)
60. Li, X., Wang, W., Hu, X., Yang, J.: Selective kernel networks. In: Proceedings of the IEEE/CVF Conference on Computer Vision and Pattern Recognition, pp. 510–519 (2019)
61. Chen, Y., Kalantidis, Y., Li, J., Yan, S., Feng, J.: Aˆ 2-nets: double attention networks. In: Proceedings of the Advances in Neural Information Processing Systems, vol. 31 (2018)
62. Dai, T., Cai, J., Zhang, Y., Xia, S.-T., Zhang, L.: Second-order attention network for single image super-resolution. In: Proceedings of the IEEE/CVF Conference on Computer Vision and Pattern Recognition, pp. 11065–11074 (2019)
63. Choi, M., Kim, H., Han, B., Xu, N., Lee, K.M.: Channel attention is all you need for video frame interpolation. In: Proceedings of the AAAI Conference on Artificial Intelligence, vol. 34, pp. 10663–10671 (2020)
64. Fu, J., Liu, J., Tian, H., Li, Y., Bao, Y., Fang, Z., Lu, H.: Dual attention network for scene segmentation. In: Proceedings of the IEEE/CVF Conference on Computer Vision and Pattern Recognition, pp. 3146–3154 (2019)
65. Shaw, P., Uszkoreit, J., Vaswani, A.: Self-attention with relative position representations. arXiv:1803.02155 (2018)
66. Wang, S., Li, B.Z., Khabsa, M., Fang, H., Ma, H.: Linformer: self-attention with linear complexity. arXiv:2006.04768 (2020)
67. Wang, X., Girshick, R., Gupta, A., He, K.: Non-local neural networks. In: Proceedings of the IEEE Conference on Computer Vision and Pattern Recognition, pp. 7794–7803 (2018)
68. Pham, N.-Q., Nguyen, T.-S., Niehues, J., Müller, M., Stüker, S., Waibel, A.: Very deep self-attention networks for end-to-end speech recognition. arXiv:1904.13377 (2019)
69. Zhang, H., Goodfellow, I., Metaxas, D., Odena, A.: Self-attention generative adversarial networks. In: Proceedings of the International Conference on Machine Learning. The Proceedings of Machine Learning Research, pp. 7354–7363 (2019)
70. Wang, L., Huang, Y., Hou, Y., Zhang, S., Shan, J.: Graph attention convolution for point cloud semantic segmentation. In: Proceedings of the IEEE/CVF Conference on Computer Vision and Pattern Recognition, pp. 10296–10305 (2019)

71. Sun, Y., Wang, Y., Liu, Z., Siegel, J., Sarma, S.: Pointgrow: autoregressively learned point cloud generation with self-attention. In: Proceedings of the IEEE/CVF Winter Conference on Applications of Computer Vision, pp. 61–70 (2020)

72. Zheng, C., Fan, X., Wang, C., Qi, J.: GMAN: a graph multi-attention network for traffic prediction. In: Proceedings of the AAAI Conference on Artificial Intelligence, vol. 34, pp. 1234–1241 (2020)

73. Devlin, J., Chang, M.-W., Lee, K., Toutanova, K.: Bert: pre-training of deep bidirectional transformers for language understanding. arXiv:1810.04805 (2018)

74. Dosovitskiy, A., Beyer, L., Kolesnikov, A., Weissenborn, D., Zhai, X., Unterthiner, T., Dehghani, M., Minderer, M., Heigold, G., Gelly, S., et al.: An image is worth 16x16 words: transformers for image recognition at scale. arXiv:2010.11929 (2020)

75. Radford, A., Kim, J.W., Hallacy, C., Ramesh, A., Goh, G., Agarwal, S., Sastry, G., Askell, A., Mishkin, P., Clark, J., et al.: Learning transferable visual models from natural language supervision. In: Proceedings of the International Conference on Machine Learning. The Proceedings of Machine Learning Research, pp. 8748–8763 (2021)

Chapter 4
Memory-Based DCNs

Abstract This chapter first provides a brief overview of memory-based Deep Cognitive Networks (DCNs). Then, representative models from two aspects in terms of short-term memory and long-term memory are introduced and analyzed, as well as their relation to important theories, computational models and experimental evidences in cognitive psychology. At last, this chapter is briefly summarized.

Keywords Memory modeling · Working memory · Semantic memory

4.1 Overview

Similar to the attention-based DCNs, a great number of memory-based DCNs [1–3] are also proposed. Inspired by the memory in human brains, many memory-based DCNs design various memory modules to store useful or historical information that can be later reused. Therefore, they can well deal with the issue of long-range temporal dependency such as in video captioning, machine translation and action recognition, as well as the issue of rare content recognition such as in few-shot image classification and open-set object detection. In Table 4.1, we mainly focus on two classes of memory-based DCNs: short-term memory and long-term memory, and their five sub-classes: working memory, short-term and long-term memory, episodic memory, conceptual memory and semantic memory. The representative memory-based DCNs include Neural Turing Machine [1], Long Short-Term Memory [4], Memory Network [2], Prototypical Network [3] and Multimodal Knowledge Graph [5]. We also elaborate their related important theories, computational models and experimental evidences in cognitive psychology. The corresponding details will be explained in the following.

Table 4.1 The taxonomy of memory-based DCNs

Class	Sub-class	Representative DCN	Theory, model and evidence
Short-term memory	Working memory	Neural turing machine [1], Differential neural computer [6]	Baddeley-Hitch model [7], Atkinson-Shiffrin model [8]
	Short-term and long-term memory	Long short-term memory [4], gated recurrent unit [9]	
Long-term memory	Episodic memory	Memory network [2], end-to-end memory network [10]	Episodic memory and semantic memory [11], dual coding of knowledge [12]
	Conceptual memory	Prototypical network [3], multimodal aligned conceptual knowledge [13]	
	Semantic memory	Multimodal knowledge graph [5]	

4.2 Short-Term Memory

In cognitive psychology, short-term memory [14] usually has a very limited storage capacity that can only hold perceived information temporarily. For example, short-term memory is usually used to hold a phone number that has just been told. Next, we mainly introduce two sub-classes of short-term memory including working memory and short-term and long-term memory.

4.2.1 Working Memory

In cognitive psychology, working memory, i.e., the Baddeley-Hitch Model [7], can be regarded as an improved version of short-term memory, which can additionally manipulate the stored information for the following processes of reasoning and decision. The Baddeley-Hitch Model has three key components: (1) a phonological loop, which stores sound or phonological information, (2) a visuo-spatial sketchpad, which stores visual information for manipulation, and (3) a central executive, which controls and regulates the whole process of information storage and manipulation.

In 2014, Graves et al. [1] proposed Neural Turing Machine (NTM), as shown in Fig. 4.1, which is one of the most influential memory-based DCNs. Similar to the Baddeley-Hitch Model, NTM also includes a controller that can receive external inputs and interact with the memory content. The major difference is that the NTM only has unimodal memory rather than bimodal memories. During the memory read and write processes, there are two kinds of access mechanisms in terms of content-

Fig. 4.1 Illustration of neural turing machine (NTM). The NTM has a controller that receives external inputs and generates the corresponding outputs. The controller can produce read and write heads, which are used to selectively read out and updated the memory content. Figure is from [1]

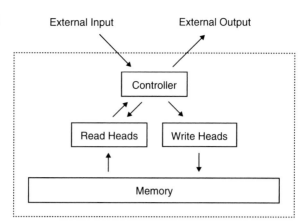

based and location-based. The whole model parameters are differentiable, so it can be optimized based on gradient descent in an end-to-end manner. Later, Graves et al. [6] extended the NTM to Differential Neural Computer (DNC), which has more advanced memory access strategies and can better deal with more complicated tasks such as question answering, graph traversal and logical planning.

The NTM attracts much attention and its many extensions are very interesting. For example, Kurach et al. [15] proposed a neural random access machine, which has discrete pointers and variable-size random-access memory. Rae et al. [16] presented a sparse access memory that can alleviate the issue of poor scaling as the amount of memory grows. Considering that the NTM only has linearly organized memory, Zhang et al. [17] and Parisotto and Salakhutdinov [18] proposed different nonlinear structured memories and achieved better performance. Wang et al. [19] proposed a multimodal version of NTM, in which the memory is shared among visual and textual information. NTM and its variants are very useful in many applications. The representative ones are: (1) capturing long-range temporal dependency in video captioning [19] and object tracking [20], and (2) retaining and reusing rare content in meta-learning [21] and image-text matching [22, 23].

In 2020, Baddeley [24] extended the original Baddeley-Hitch Model by adding the fourth component namely Episodic Buffer, which is able to temporarily store the information of episodes or scenes. Accordingly, there are also several models developing similar modules that storing different types of episodic and scene-level information such as semantic word [25], topic or history [26], and indoor scene [27].

4.2.2   Short-Term and Long-Term Memory

In cognitive psychology, the Atkinson-Shiffrin Model [8] describes the relation between short-term memory and long-term memory, which consists of three important components: (1) sensory register, which perceives external information,

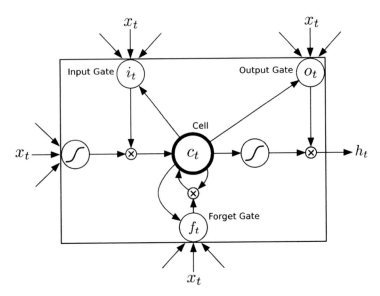

Fig. 4.2 Illustration of long short-term memory (LSTM). The LSTM is composed of an input vector x_t, an output vector h_t, a memory cell c_t, an input gate i_t, an output gate o_t and a forget gate f_t, where t is the indext of timestep. Figure is from [28]

(2) short-term memory, which receives and stores information from both sensor register and long-term memory, and (3) long-term memory, which stores rehearsed information in the short-term memory indefinitely. As shown in Fig. 4.2, the well-known Long Short-Term Memory (LSTM) [4] also considers the relation of two kinds of memories, which includes a memory cell to store long-term stable information and network parameters to store short-term temporary information, respectively. Note that LSTM is also related to the working memory, because its memory cell is manipulated by three gates controlling the information flow in and out of the memory cell, which is similar to the central executive in the working memory.

The LSTM has been widely studied from both aspects of model extension and application. There are many representative and influential extensions of LSTM. For example, Chung et al. [9] proposed a light version of LSTM named Gated Recurrent Unit (GRU), which achieves similar performance compared with LSTM but has fewer learning parameters. Tai et al. [29] proposed a tree-structured LSTM that can well model tree structures in the natural language. Kiros et al. [30] combined the LSTM with encoder-decoder architecture and proposed skip-thought vectors, which can encode arbitrary sentences. Srivastava et al. [31] transferred the idea of LSTM to conventional CNNs to address their gradient vanishing and exploring problems.

Up to now, the LSTM and its extensions are still golden approaches in various applications such as speech recognition [28], image captioning [32], action recognition [33], question answering [34], text classification [35], etc.

4.3 Long-Term Memory

Many experimental evidences show that elaborative rehearsal can help move the stored information from short-term memory to long-term memory [36, 37]. In contrast to the short-term memory, long-term memory has a unlimited storage capability that can maintain its stored information for long periods. In cognitive psychology, there are two main types of long-term memory: explicit (declarative) memory [38] and implicit (non-declarative) memory [39]. In 1972, Tulving [11] further proposed two types of explicit memories: (1) episodic memory, which stores specific personal experiences and previous events, and (2) semantic memory, which stores factual information and semantic concepts. Different from explicit memory, the implicit memory is usually non-conscious but can affect thoughts and behaviours. Since existing memory-based DCNs mostly model the explicit memory, we only introduce three sub-classes of the explicit memory as follows.

4.3.1 Episodic Memory

To our knowledge, Weston et al. [2] proposed the first model of episodic memory named Memory Network (MN), which contains a memory component storing episodic information represented as an array of representations. As shown in Fig. 4.3, it has another four components that interact with the memory component: (1) input feature map, which converts an input to its representation, (2) generalization, which updates the old memory based on the input representation, (3) output feature map, which produces an output representation by combining the input representation and current memory, and (4) response, which converts the output representation to the desired response. The effectiveness of MN is first demonstrated in a large-scale question answering task, in which the memory component is used to provide historical or prior information.

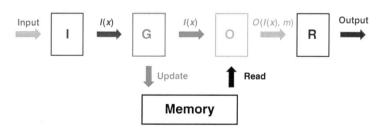

Fig. 4.3 Illustration of memory network (MN). The model is composed of five components, in which I obtains the input representation $I(x)$, G updates the memory, O combines the $I(x)$ with the read out memory m, and R generates desired output based on the $O(I(x), m)$

Later, three important MN extensions were proposed. The first one is End-to-End MN [10], which requires much less supervision during training than the original MN. In particular, it introduces the RNN-like architecture to recurrently read the memory component multiple times, so that the whole model can be efficiently trained in an end-to-end manner. The End-to-End MN has been widely used in many applications including text classification [40] and dialogue generation [41]. The second one is Dynamic MN proposed by Kumar et al. [42], which uses advanced sequence models for input and response components. It is motivated by the fact that the original MN cannot well capture the temporal positional information of support sentences. In particular, it represents each sentence as a set of word-level features and treats all the sentences sequentially. The Dynamic MN is more suitable for the applications of visual question answering [43] and motion detection [44]. The third one is Key-Value MN proposed by Miller et al. [45], which designs the memory component as key-value pairs and generalizes the original MN to better deal with external knowledge graphs. For the task of question answering, the model regards questions as queries and finds the most related keys in the memory. Then the corresponding values are summed and returned to predict the final answer. As a result, the Key-Value MN is more suitable for the applications based on the knowledge graphs such as rare event analysis [46] and clinical diagnostic inference [47].

In addition to the MN and its variants, there is also another kind of episodic memory model named Memory Bank (MB) [48]. It stores representations of all samples in the dataset, which can be used for reference to improve the feature learning. He et al. [49] improved the MB as Momentum Contrast (MoCo), which is very useful for contrastive learning. Later, Bulat et al. [50] and Sun et al. [51] proposed more extensions from aspects of large mini-batch training, hard negative mining and multi-level aggregation.

4.3.2 Conceptual Memory

In cognitive psychology, a prototype is usually considered as a mental representation for a semantic concept, which contains the most salient features related to the concept. Thus, prototype learning can be regarded as a representative approach for modeling concepts in the semantic memory [11], i.e., conceptual memory. Even before the rise of deep learning, prototype learning has been widely studied. Kohonen [52] proposed an early work of Learning Vector Quantization (LVQ), which is later extended in two directions. The first one focuses on manually designing better rules to update prototypes [53], while the second one focuses on directly learning prototypes in a parametric manner [54].

Later in 2017, Snell et al. [3] proposed Prototypical Network (PN), which implements the idea of prototype learning based on deep learning, as shown in Fig. 4.4. The PN uses a neural network to map input samples to their embeddings, and then computes each concept's prototype by averaging related sample embeddings. As

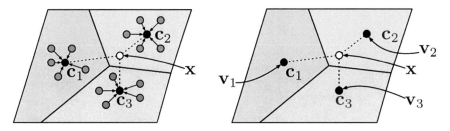

Fig. 4.4 Illustration of prototypical network (PN) in few-shot learning and zero-shot learning scenarios. Left: each few-shot prototype c_k for each class is computed by averaging the related sample embeddings. Right: each zero-shot prototype c_k is obtained by using the embedding of class meta-data v_k. In either case, an embedded sample x can be classified by comparing it with all the prototypes to find the nearest one. Figure is from [3]

a result, the PN can obtain pairs of semantic concepts and prototypes. It can be regarded as a rough simulation of semantic memory, since concepts and prototypes can be adaptively added, deleted or updated like memory content in human brains. In this direction, there are many effective extensions from the perspectives of convolutional prototype learning [55], combination of prototype and concept [56] and hyperspherical prototype learning [57]. In addition, Huang et al. [13] designed Multimodal Aligned Conceptual Knowledge (MACK) that can learn multimodal paired prototypes, which is inspired by the evidence of Dual Coding of Knowledge in human brains [12]. Excepting for the few-shot learning, the PN and its variants are also widely used in other applications such as emotion recognition [58], speaker verification [59] and temporal action localization [60].

4.3.3 Semantic Memory

In addition to the concepts, semantic memory [11] also stores another kind of general world knowledge namely facts. Knowledge Graph (KG) [61, 62] is the most representative method for modeling the semantic memory. As shown in Fig. 4.5, a concept in a KG is represented as an entity, and a fact is represented as an entity-based triple in the form of (head entity, relation, tail entity), which indicates that two entities are related by the relation. Similar to the knowledge organization in human brains, entities and triples in the KG are organized in a graph structure, which can be adaptively added, deleted or updated.

Up to now, many well-known KGs are proposed. For example, DBpedia [64] is one of the earliest KGs that automatically extracts world knowledge from information boxes of Wikipedia, which totally contains about 900 million triple-structured knowledge in 2021. Later, YAGO [65] combined DBpedia with a lexical KG namely WordNet [66], which has the ability of logical reasoning. Recently, multimodal versions of KGs have drawn much attention, most of which extend

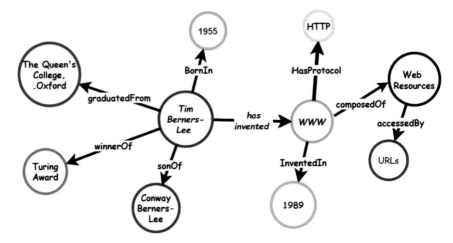

Fig. 4.5 Illustration of knowledge graph (KG) in terms of entities and relations. We can infer some facts (triples) such as (Tim Berners-Lee, has invented, WWW), (WWW, is composed of, Web Resources), and (Tim Berners-Lee, is winner of, Turing Award). Figure is from [63]

existing linguistic ones by adding the visual information. For example, based on Freebase [67] and DBpedia, Multimodal Knowledge Graph (MKG) [5] contains more than 30,000 entities and more than 810,000 triples, among which only about 18% entities are not related to images.

KGs are very effective in organizing structured knowledge, but it is difficult for users to directly operate on symbolic entities and triples in practical applications. To alleviate this issue, various KG embedding methods [68] based on deep learning are proposed, which can embed entities and triples into continuous vector spaces. Among them, representative methods are TransE [69] and its variants including TransH [70] and TransR [71]. Up to now, many models have been proposed for diverse KG-based tasks including relation extraction [72], entity classification [73] and entity disambiguation [74].

4.4   Brief Summary

Up to now, many memory-based DCNs are proposed to model the working memory, episodic memory and semantic memory, which have achieved great performance improvements in practical applications such as meta-learning and question answering. Different from them, the modeling of implicit memory is much less explored. In fact, the implicit memory plays an essential role in our daily activities such as singing a song and riding a bike, which helps us to perform skills automatically and unconsciously.

References

1. Graves, A., Wayne, G., Danihelka, I.: Neural turing machines. arXiv:1410.5401 (2014)
2. Weston, J., Chopra, S., Bordes, A.: Memory networks. arXiv:1410.3916 (2014)
3. Snell, J., Swersky, K., Zemel, R.: Prototypical networks for few-shot learning. In: Proceedings of the Advances in Neural Information Processing Systems, vol. 30 (2017)
4. Hochreiter, S., Schmidhuber, J.: Long short-term memory. Neural Comput. 9(8), 1735–1780 (1997)
5. Liu, Y., Li, H., Garcia-Duran, A., Niepert, M., Onoro-Rubio, D., Rosenblum, D.S.: MMKG: multi-modal knowledge graphs. In: European Semantic Web Conference, pp. 459–474. Springer, Berlin (2019)
6. Graves, A., Wayne, G., Reynolds, M., Harley, T., Danihelka, I., Grabska-Barwińska, A., Colmenarejo, S. G., Grefenstette, E., Ramalho, T., Agapiou, J., et al.: Hybrid computing using a neural network with dynamic external memory. Nature 538(7626), 471–476 (2016)
7. Baddeley, A.D., Hitch, G.: Working memory. In: Psychology of Learning and Motivation, vol. 8, pp. 47–89. Elsevier, Amsterdam (1974)
8. Atkinson, R.C., Shiffrin, R.M.: Human memory: a proposed system and its control processes. In: Psychology of Learning and Motivation, vol. 2, pp. 89–195. Elsevier, Amsterdam (1968)
9. Chung, J., Gulcehre, C., Cho, K., Bengio, Y.: Empirical evaluation of gated recurrent neural networks on sequence modeling. arXiv:1412.3555 (2014)
10. Sukhbaatar, S., Weston, J., Fergus, R., et al.: End-to-end memory networks. In: Proceedings of the Advances in Neural Information Processing Systems, vol. 28 (2015)
11. Tulving, E.: Episodic and semantic memory. Organ. Memory 381–403 (1972). http://alumni.media.mit.edu/~jorkin/generals/papers/Tulving_memory.pdf
12. Bi, Y.: Dual coding of knowledge in the human brain. Trends Cognit. Sci. 25(10), 883–895 (2021)
13. Huang, Y., Wang, Y., Zeng, Y., Wang, L.: MACK: multimodal aligned conceptual knowledge for unpaired image-text matching. In: Proceedings of the Advances in Neural Information Processing Systems (2022)
14. Miller, G.A.: The magical number seven, plus or minus two: some limits on our capacity for processing information. Psychol. Rev. 63(2), 81 (1956)
15. Kurach, K., Andrychowicz, M., Sutskever, I.: Neural random-access machines. arXiv:1511.06392 (2015)
16. Rae, J., Hunt, J.J., Danihelka, I., Harley, T., Senior, A.W., Wayne, G., Graves, A., Lillicrap, T.: Scaling memory-augmented neural networks with sparse reads and writes. In: Proceedings of the Advances in Neural Information Processing Systems, vol. 29 (2016)
17. Zhang, W., Yu, Y., Zhou, B.: Structured memory for neural turing machines. arXiv:1510.03931 (2015)
18. Parisotto, E., Salakhutdinov, R.: Neural map: structured memory for deep reinforcement learning. arXiv:1702.08360 (2017)
19. Wang, J., Wang, W., Huang, Y., Wang, L., Tan, T.: M3: multimodal memory modelling for video captioning. In: Proceedings of the IEEE Conference on Computer Vision and Pattern Recognition, pp. 7512–7520 (2018)
20. Yang, T., Chan, A.B.: Learning dynamic memory networks for object tracking. In: Proceedings of the European Conference on Computer Vision, pp. 152–167 (2018)
21. Santoro, A., Bartunov, S., Botvinick, M., Wierstra, D., Lillicrap, T.: Meta-learning with memory-augmented neural networks. In: Proceedings of the International Conference on Machine Learning. The Proceedings of Machine Learning Research, pp. 1842–1850 (2016)
22. Huang, Y., Wang, L.: ACMM: aligned cross-modal memory for few-shot image and sentence matching. In: Proceedings of the IEEE/CVF International Conference on Computer Vision, pp. 5774–5783 (2019)
23. Huang, Y., Wang, J., Wang, L.: Few-shot image and sentence matching via aligned cross-modal memory. IEEE Trans. Pattern Anal. Mach. Intell. 44(6), 2968–2983 (2021)

24. Baddeley, A.: The episodic buffer: a new component of working memory? Trends Cognit. Sci. **4**(11), 417–423 (2000)
25. Yang, G.R., Ganichev, I., Wang, X.-J., Shlens, J., Sussillo, D.: A dataset and architecture for visual reasoning with a working memory. In: Proceedings of the European Conference on Computer Vision, pp. 714–731 (2018)
26. Yi, X., Sun, M., Li, R., Yang, Z.: Chinese poetry generation with a working memory model. arXiv:1809.04306 (2018)
27. Wang, H., Wang, W., Liang, W., Xiong, C., Shen, J.: Structured scene memory for vision-language navigation. In: Proceedings of the IEEE/CVF Conference on Computer Vision and Pattern Recognition, pp. 8455–8464 (2021)
28. Graves, A., Mohamed, A.-R., Hinton, G.: Speech recognition with deep recurrent neural networks. In: Proceedings of the IEEE International Conference on Acoustics, Speech and Signal Processing, pp. 6645–6649. IEEE, Piscataway (2013)
29. Tai, K.S., Socher, R., Manning, C.D.: Improved semantic representations from tree-structured long short-term memory networks. arXiv:1503.00075 (2015)
30. Kiros, R., Zhu, Y., Salakhutdinov, R.R., Zemel, R., Urtasun, R., Torralba, A., Fidler, S.: Skip-thought vectors. In: Proceedings of the Advances in Neural Information Processing Systems, vol. 28 (2015)
31. Srivastava, R.K., Greff, K., Schmidhuber, J.: Training very deep networks. In: Proceedings of the Advances in Neural Information Processing Systems, vol. 28 (2015)
32. Vinyals, O., Toshev, A., Bengio, S., Erhan, D.: Show and tell: a neural image caption generator. In: Proceedings of the IEEE Conference on Computer Vision and Pattern Recognition, pp. 3156–3164 (2015)
33. Donahue, J., Anne Hendricks, L., Guadarrama, S., Rohrbach, M., Venugopalan, S., Saenko, K., Darrell, T.: Long-term recurrent convolutional networks for visual recognition and description. In: Proceedings of the IEEE Conference on Computer Vision and Pattern Recognition, pp. 2625–2634 (2015)
34. Hermann, K.M., Kocisky, T., Grefenstette, E., Espeholt, L., Kay, W., Suleyman, M., Blunsom, P.: Teaching machines to read and comprehend. In: Advances in Neural Information Processing Systems, vol. 28 (2015)
35. Liu, P., Qiu, X., Chen, X., Wu, S., Huang, X.-J.: Multi-timescale long short-term memory neural network for modelling sentences and documents. In: Proceedings of the Conference on Empirical Methods in Natural Language Processing, pp. 2326–2335 (2015)
36. Goldstein, E.B.: Cognitive Psychology: Connecting Mind, Research and Everyday Experience. Cengage Learning (2014)
37. Reisberg, D.: Cognition: Exploring the Science of the Mind. WW Norton & Company, New York (2010)
38. Ullman, M.T.: Contributions of memory circuits to language: the declarative/procedural model. Cognition **92**(1–2), 231–270 (2004)
39. Schacter, D.L.: Implicit memory: history and current status. J. Exp. Psychol. Learn. Memory Cognit. **13**(3), 501 (1987)
40. Zeng, J., Li, J., Song, Y., Gao, C., Lyu, M.R., King, I.: Topic memory networks for short text classification. arXiv:1809.03664 (2018)
41. Chen, H., Ren, Z., Tang, J., Zhao, Y.E., Yin, D.: Hierarchical variational memory network for dialogue generation. In: Proceedings of the World Wide Web Conference, pp. 1653–1662 (2018)
42. Kumar, A., Irsoy, O., Ondruska, P., Iyyer, M., Bradbury, J., Gulrajani, I., Zhong, V., Paulus, R., Socher, R.: Ask me anything: dynamic memory networks for natural language processing. In: Proceedings of the International Conference on Machine Learning. The Proceedings of Machine Learning Research, pp. 1378–1387 (2016)
43. Xiong, C., Merity, S., Socher, R.: Dynamic memory networks for visual and textual question answering. In: International Conference on Machine Learning. The Proceedings of Machine Learning Research, pp. 2397–2406 (2016)

44. Hazarika, D., Poria, S., Mihalcea, R., Cambria, E., Zimmermann, R.: ICON: interactive conversational memory network for multimodal emotion detection. In: Proceedings of the Conference on Empirical Methods in Natural Language Processing, pp. 2594–2604 (2018)
45. Miller, A., Fisch, A., Dodge, J., Karimi, A.-H., Bordes, A., Weston, J.: Key-value memory networks for directly reading documents. arXiv:1606.03126 (2016)
46. Kaiser, Ł., Nachum, O., Roy, A., Bengio, S.: Learning to remember rare events. arXiv:1703.03129 (2017)
47. Prakash, A., Zhao, S., Hasan, S.A., Datla, V., Lee, K., Qadir, A., Liu, J., Farri, O.: Condensed memory networks for clinical diagnostic inferencing. In: Proceedings of the AAAI Conference on Artificial Intelligence (2017)
48. Wu, Z., Xiong, Y., Yu, S.X., Lin, D.: Unsupervised feature learning via non-parametric instance discrimination. In: Proceedings of the IEEE Conference on Computer Vision and Pattern Recognition, pp. 3733–3742 (2018)
49. He, K., Fan, H., Wu, Y., Xie, S., Girshick, R.: Momentum contrast for unsupervised visual representation learning. In: Proceedings of the IEEE/CVF Conference on Computer Vision and Pattern Recognition, pp. 9729–9738 (2020)
50. Bulat, A., Sánchez-Lozano, E., Tzimiropoulos, G.: Improving memory banks for unsupervised learning with large mini-batch, consistency and hard negative mining. In: Proceedings of the IEEE International Conference on Acoustics, Speech and Signal Processing, pp. 1695–1699. IEEE, Piscataway (2021)
51. Sun, G., Hua, Y., Hu, G., Robertson, N.: MAMBA: multi-level aggregation via memory bank for video object detection. In: Proceedings of the AAAI Conference on Artificial Intelligence, vol. 35, pp. 2620–2627 (2021)
52. Kohonen, T.: The self-organizing map. Proc. IEEE **78**(9), 1464–1480 (1990)
53. Kohonen, T.: Improved versions of learning vector quantization. In: Proceedings of the International Joint Conference on Neural Networks, pp. 545–550. IEEE, Piscataway (1990)
54. Sato, A., Yamada, K.: Generalized learning vector quantization. In: Proceedings of the Advances in Neural Information Processing Systems, vol. 8 (1995)
55. Yang, H.-M., Zhang, X.-Y., Yin, F., Liu, C.-L.: Robust classification with convolutional prototype learning. In: Proceedings of the IEEE Conference on Computer Vision and Pattern Recognition, pp. 3474–3482 (2018)
56. Xing, C., Rostamzadeh, N., Oreshkin, B., O Pinheiro, P.O.: Adaptive cross-modal few-shot learning. In: Proceedings of the Advances in Neural Information Processing Systems, vol. 32 (2019)
57. Mettes, P., van der Pol, E., Snoek, C.: Hyperspherical prototype networks. In: Proceedings of the Advances in Neural Information Processing Systems, vol. 32 (2019)
58. Soumya, K., Palaniswamy, S.: Emotion recognition from partially occluded facial images using prototypical networks. In: Proceedings of the International Conference on Innovative Mechanisms for Industry Applications, pp. 491–497. IEEE, Piscataway (2020)
59. Ko, T., Chen, Y., Li, Q.: Prototypical networks for small footprint text-independent speaker verification. In: Proceedings of the IEEE International Conference on Acoustics, Speech and Signal Processing, pp. 6804–6808. IEEE, Piscataway (2020)
60. Huang, L., Huang, Y., Ouyang, W., Wang, L.: Relational prototypical network for weakly supervised temporal action localization. In: Proceedings of the AAAI Conference on Artificial Intelligence, vol. 34, pp. 11053–11060 (2020)
61. Hogan, A., Blomqvist, E., Cochez, M., d'Amato, C., Melo, G.D., Gutierrez, C., Kirrane, S., Gayo, J.E.L., Navigli, R., Neumaier, S., et al.: Knowledge graphs. ACM Comput. Surv. **54**(4), 1–37 (2021)
62. Singhal, A., et al.: Introducing the knowledge graph: things, not strings. Official Google Blog **5**, 16 (2012)
63. Abu-Salih, B.: Domain-specific knowledge graphs: a survey. J. Netw. Comput. Appl. **185**, 103076 (2021)
64. Auer, S., Bizer, C., Kobilarov, G., Lehmann, J., Cyganiak, R., Ives, Z.: DBpedia: a nucleus for a web of open data. In: Semantic Web, pp. 722–735. Springer, Berlin (2007)

65. Suchanek, F.M., Kasneci, G., Weikum, G.: Yago: a core of semantic knowledge. In: Proceedings of the International Conference on World Wide Web, pp. 697–706 (2007)
66. Miller, G.A.: Wordnet: a lexical database for english. Commun. ACM **38**(11), 39–41 (1995)
67. Bollacker, K., Evans, C., Paritosh, P., Sturge, T., Taylor, J.: Freebase: a collaboratively created graph database for structuring human knowledge. In: Proceedings of the ACM SIGMOD International Conference on Management of Data, pp. 1247–1250 (2008)
68. Wang, Q., Mao, Z., Wang, B., Guo, L.: Knowledge graph embedding: a survey of approaches and applications. IEEE Trans. Knowl. Data Eng. **29**(12), 2724–2743 (2017)
69. Bordes, A., Usunier, N., Garcia-Duran, A., Weston, J., Yakhnenko, O.: Translating embeddings for modeling multi-relational data. In: Proceedings of the Advances in Neural Information Processing Systems, vol. 26 (2013)
70. Wang, Z., Zhang, J., Feng, J., Chen, Z.: Knowledge graph embedding by translating on hyperplanes. In: Proceedings of the AAAI Conference on Artificial Intelligence, vol. 28 (2014)
71. Lin, Y., Liu, Z., Sun, M., Liu, Y., Zhu, X.: Learning entity and relation embeddings for knowledge graph completion. In: Proceedings of the AAAI Conference on Artificial Intelligence (2015)
72. Nguyen, T.H., Grishman, R.: Relation extraction: perspective from convolutional neural networks. In: Proceedings of the Workshop on Vector Space Modeling for Natural Language Processing, pp. 39–48 (2015)
73. Li, J., Sun, A., Han, J., Li, C.: A survey on deep learning for named entity recognition. IEEE Trans. Knowl. Data Eng. **34**(1), 50–70 (2020)
74. Ganea, O.-E., Hofmann, T.: Deep joint entity disambiguation with local neural attention. arXiv:1704.04920 (2017)

Chapter 5
Reasoning-Based DCNs

Abstract This chapter first provides a brief overview of reasoning-based Deep Cognitive Networks (DCNs). Then, representative models from two aspects in terms of analogical reasoning and deductive reasoning are introduced and analyzed, as well as their relation to important theories, computational models and experimental evidences in cognitive psychology. At last, this chapter is briefly summarized.

Keywords Reasoning modeling · Abstract reasoning · Compositional reasoning

5.1 Overview

Reasoning is the process of performing inference based on existing premises or knowledge to draw conclusions. Compared with attention and memory, reasoning is much more complicated and the number of reasoning-based DCNs is smaller. In Table 5.1, we mainly focus on two classes of reasoning-based DCNs: analogical reasoning and deductive reasoning, and their four sub-classes: memory reasoning, abstract reasoning, compositional reasoning and programmed reasoning. The representative reasoning-based DCNs include Memory Network [1], IQ of Deep Learning [2], Neural Module Network [3] and Neural Programmer [4]. We also elaborate their related important theories, computational models and experimental evidences in cognitive psychology. The corresponding details will be explained in the following.

5.2 Analogical Reasoning

Analogical reasoning attempts to understand unfamiliar targets (e.g., situations, exemplars and domains) by referring to familiar sources based on their similarity. Analogical reasoning could be regarded a weaker form of inductive reasoning, since inductive reasoning usually requires a larger number of samples to reason [19, 20].

Y. Huang, L. Wang, *Deep Cognitive Networks*, SpringerBriefs in Computer Science,
https://doi.org/10.1007/978-981-99-0279-8_5

Table 5.1 The taxonomy of reasoning-based DCNs

Class	Sub-class	Representative DCN	Theory, model and evidence
Analogical reasoning	Memory reasoning	Memory network [1], End-to-end memory network [5]	Structure mapping theory [6, 7], learning and inference with schemas and analogies [8, 9]
	Abstract reasoning	IQ of deep learning [2], relation network [10]	
Deductive reasoning	Compositional reasoning	Neural module network [3], routing network [11]	Modular organization and structure [12, 13], symbolic numerical process [14, 15], mental logic theory [16, 17]
	Programmed reasoning	Neural programmer [4], neural programmer-interpreter[18]	

In the following, we discuss two representative sub-classes of analogical reasoning: memory reasoning and abstract reasoning.

5.2.1   Memory Reasoning

Generally in cognitive psychology, there are five key steps in an analogical reasoning process [21], which include: (1) retrieval, which retrieves a similar and familiar source in the memory by regarding the target as query, (2) mapping, which maps characteristics of the retrieved source to the target, (3) evaluation, which evaluates whether the analogy is useful or not, (4) abstraction, which extracts the common structural information of the source and target, and (5) prediction, which generates predictions about the target.

The five-step process is similar to the reasoning process in current memory-based DCNs [1, 5, 22–26]. In Fig. 5.1, we take the End-to-End Memory Network [5] for example. When applying it to the task of visual question answering, the representation of a given question is first used to retrieve similar memory items. This corresponds to the first step of retrieval mentioned above. Then, the representations of similar memory items are extracted and mapped to that of the question. This corresponds to the second step of mapping. At last, the combined representation is used for predicting the desired answer, which corresponds to the fifth step of prediction. These three steps constitute a complete process of one-round memory reasoning. In fact, most existing memory-based DCNs usually perform the one-round memory reasoning multiple times, in which the output of last-round reasoning is taken as the input of next-round reasoning. Such multi-round reasoning implicitly

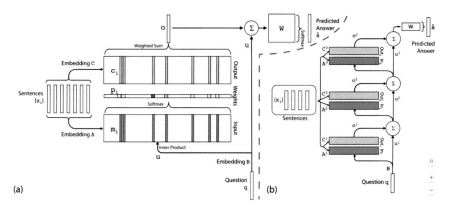

Fig. 5.1 Illustration of end-to-end memory network for the task of visual question answering. (**a**): One-round memory reasoning. (**b**): Three-round memory reasoning. Details are explained in Sect. 5.2.1. Figure is from [5]

simulates the third and fourth steps of evaluation and abstraction mentioned above, which is able to predict more accurate answers.

Among the five steps, the first two steps of retrieval and mapping are more important. There are two related theories namely Structure Mapping Theory (SMT) [6, 7] and Learning and Inference with Schemas and Analogies (LISA) [8, 9]. They both argue that structural similarity is very important during the two steps, i.e., relation among entities in the targets or sources, rather than intrinsic features of the entities [27]. However, in existing memory-based DCNs, the modeling of structural similarity is seldom explored. Instead, most of them choose to use either content-based similarity [28, 29], location-based similarity [24] or usage-based similarity [30], which are mainly determined by the non-structural information.

5.2.2 Abstract Reasoning

In 1938, John Raven [31] proposed the well-known human IQ test: Raven's Progressive Matrices (RPM). As shown in Fig. 5.2, each problem is composed of 8 images in an uncompleted 3 × 3 matrix and multiple candidate answer images. One has to analogically reason the relation among these images based on abstract structures, e.g., shapes, positions and angles, to finally select the most suitable candidate image to complete the matrix. To deal with the problem of abstract reasoning, many effective computational models in cognitive psychology were proposed [32–34], which demonstrated that the problem can be addressed by comparing images via the modeling of structural mapping. But most of them made a less practical assumption that symbolic image representations are available.

Recently, a few researchers have tried to apply deep learning models to deal with the problem. Hoshen and Werman [2] made an early attempt to test the IQ of deep

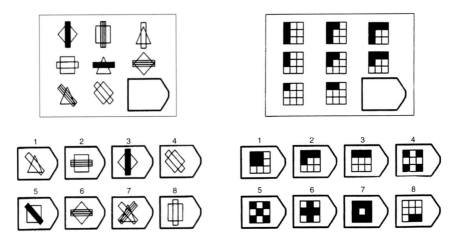

Fig. 5.2 Illustration of two examples of Raven's progressive matrices (RPM)

learning models, in which CNNs are used to take multiple raw images as inputs and predict the candidate image by reasoning the inter-image relation. Battett et al. [10] and Zhang et al. [35] proposed two large-scale datasets containing 1.4 million and 0.4 million RPM-like problems, respectively, which greatly facilitate the end-to-end supervised learning. Later, various deep learning models were proposed to replace the CNNs for better representation learning, e.g., residual network [36], variational auto-encoder [37], dynamic tree network [35] and relation network [10].

In addition to the supervised learning, Steenbrugge et al. [37] and Van et al. [38] studied unsupervised mappings from high-dimensional feature space to factors of variation, and demonstrated that disentangled representations are helpful for the abstract reasoning. Zhuo and Kankanhalli [39] combined the supervised learning and unsupervised learning together to further improve the performance of RPM. There are also other learning methods [36, 40] based on contrastive learning and RL, which are motivated to learn abstract structures and alleviate the impact of distracting features, respectively. Recently, Ichien et al. [41] presented a comprehensive comparison between deep learning models and early computational models on visual analogy tasks. Although much progress has been achieved, the study of abstract reasoning is still in its initial stage, and there are many issues remained to be solved.

5.3   Deductive Reasoning

Inductive reasoning and deductive reasoning are two major types of reasoning in cognitive psychology. Inductive reasoning aims to obtain general principles based on premises. Different from it, deductive reasoning aims to combine the principles

and premises to get conclusions. Next, we will introduce its two sub-classes in terms
of compositional reasoning and programmed reasoning.

5.3.1   Compositional Reasoning

In cognitive psychology, there are already many experimental evidences about
Modular Organization and Structure in human brains [12, 13]. Similar idea of
compositional reasoning has been explored in artificial intelligence, which first
decomposes a reasoning task into multiple sub-tasks and then addresses them
separately with compositional modules. An early work of compositional reasoning
based on DNNs was proposed by Ronco et al. [42] in 1996, which groups different
features of an input in a self-decomposition manner.

As shown in Fig. 5.3, Andreas et al. [3] proposed one of the most representative
works namely Neural Module Network (NMN) for visual question answering. It first
parses a question into its linguistic layout and then uses it as guidance to construct
multiple neural modules. Compared with the earlier work [42], the modules in the
NMN contain reusable and semantic components that can better facilitate high-level
semantic reasoning. Different from NMN that uses rule-based layouts generated
from dependency parses, Andreas et al. [43] proposed a dynamic version of NMN
that learns to re-rank layouts from external parsers. To make the NMN end-to-end

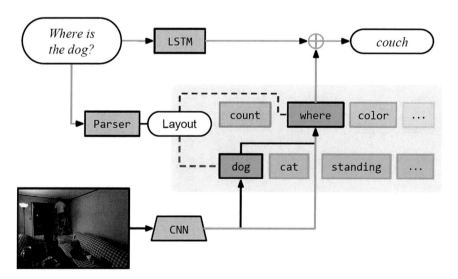

Fig. 5.3 Illustration of neural module network (NMN) for the task of visual question answering.
The NMN first uses a natural language parser to get the layout of a question, and then uses it to
build a model composed of reusable modules. At last, these modules are combined to reason on
the image to predict the final answer. Figure is from [3]

learnable, Hu et al. [44, 45] replaced the fixed parser by directly learning optimal layouts jointly with the modules. NMN and its variants have been applied to many tasks such as question answering [43], visual question answering [46], referring expression [44], visual grounding [47] and visual dialog [48].

Compositional reasoning is also related to another kind of model namely Mixtures of Experts (MoE) [49, 50]. In this model, each expert is a parameterized function with specific property, and the output is the weighted sum of all functions. Recently, it is also extended by combining deep learning models [51, 52]. In contrast to the conventional "soft" mixture, Rosenbaum et al. [11] designed a Routing Network (RN) that can combine the experts in a "hard" routing manner.

5.3.2 *Programmed Reasoning*

One major limitation of most deep learning models during reasoning is that they cannot well learn arithmetic or logical operations [53–55]. A feasible solution is program induction [56], which can alleviate the limitation by generating a language-like program for programmed reasoning. It is consistent with the evidences of Symbolic Numerical Processes in human brain [14, 15], as well as the Mental Logic Theory [16, 17], which applies syntactic rules to transform premises to conclusions in a language-like process.

To our knowledge, Neelakantan et al. [4] proposed the earliest work namely Neural Programmer (NP), as shown in Fig. 5.4. Based on a DNN, the model can adaptively induce a program consisting of a series of arithmetic and logical operations. At each timestep, it selects a particular operation to process data and then propagates the output. Another representative work is Neural Programmer-Interpreter (NPI) [18], which uses a program memory to generate new programs

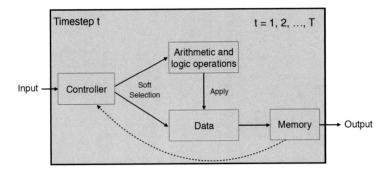

Fig. 5.4 Illustration of neural programmer (NP). The NP runs for several timesteps to induce a complex program that is composed of operations. At each timestep, the controller selects an operation, and the memory stores the output by applying the selected operation to the data. Figure is from [4]

by combining existing programs. However, the NPI learns to induce programs with too strong supervision of the entire program. To this end, some works [57, 58] have attempted to relax this limitations by weakly supervised learning. Up to now, programmed reasoning has been demonstrated to be useful for visual question answering [59], reading comprehension [60] and machine translation [61].

5.4 Brief Summary

The modeling of reasoning has just started recently, so the total number of reasoning-based DCNs is much smaller than those of attention-based DCNs and memory-based DCNs. Among all the reasoning-based DCNs, memory reasoning and compositional reasoning have attracted more attention, and been demonstrated to be effective in more applications. In addition,, encouraging progress has also been made in some particular tasks such as visual commonsense reasoning [62] and knowledge graph reasoning [63].

References

1. Weston, J., Chopra, S., Bordes, A.: Memory networks. arXiv:1410.3916 (2014)
2. Hoshen, D., Werman, M.: IQ of neural networks. arXiv:1710.01692 (2017)
3. Andreas, J., Rohrbach, M., Darrell, T., Klein, D.: Neural module networks. In: Proceedings of the IEEE Conference on Computer Vision and Pattern Recognition, pp. 39–48 (2016)
4. Neelakantan, A., Le, Q.V., Sutskever, I.: Neural programmer: inducing latent programs with gradient descent. arXiv:1511.04834 (2015)
5. Sukhbaatar, S., Weston, J., Fergus, R., et al.: End-to-end memory networks. In: Proceedings of the Advances in Neural Information Processing Systems, vol. 28 (2015)
6. Gentner, D.: Structure-mapping: a theoretical framework for analogy. Cognit. Sci. 7(2), 155–170 (1983)
7. Falkenhainer, B., Forbus, K.D., Gentner, D.: The structure-mapping engine: algorithm and examples. Artif. Intell. 41(1), 1–63 (1989)
8. Hummel, J.E., Holyoak, K.J.: Distributed representations of structure: a theory of analogical access and mapping. Psychol. Rev. 104(3), 427 (1997)
9. Hummel, J.E., Holyoak, K.J.: A symbolic-connectionist theory of relational inference and generalization. Psychol. Rev. 110(2), 220 (2003)
10. Barrett, D., Hill, F., Santoro, A., Morcos, A., Lillicrap, T.: Measuring abstract reasoning in neural networks. In: Proceedings of the International Conference on Machine Learning. The Proceedings of Machine Learning Research, pp. 511–520 (2018)
11. Rosenbaum, C., Klinger, T., Riemer, M.: Routing networks: adaptive selection of non-linear functions for multi-task learning. arXiv:1711.01239 (2017)
12. Sternberg, S.: Modular processes in mind and brain. Cognit. Neuropsychol. 28(3–4), 156–208 (2011)
13. Meunier, D., Lambiotte, R., Bullmore, E.T.: Modular and hierarchically modular organization of brain networks. Front. Neurosci. 4, 200 (2010)
14. Piazza, M., Izard, V., Pinel, P., Le Bihan, D., Dehaene, S.: Tuning curves for approximate numerosity in the human intraparietal sulcus. Neuron 44(3), 547–555 (2004)

15. Cantlon, J.F., Brannon, E.M., Carter, E.J., Pelphrey, K.A.: Functional imaging of numerical processing in adults and 4-y-old children. PLoS Biol. **4**(5), e125 (2006)
16. Johnson-Laird, P.N., Byrne, R.M.: Precis of deduction. Behav. Brain Sci. **16**(2), 323–333 (1993)
17. Johnson-Laird, P.N.: Mental models and deductive reasoning. Reason. Stud. Hum. Infer. Found. 206–222 (2008)
18. Reed, S., De Freitas, N.: Neural programmer-interpreters. arXiv:1511.06279 (2015)
19. Walton, D.N.: Argumentation schemes for argument from analogy. In: Systematic Approaches to Argument by Analogy, pp. 23–40. Springer, Berlin (2014)
20. Sloman, S.A., Lagnado, D.: The problem of induction. In: The Cambridge Handbook of Thinking and Reasoning, pp. 95–116. Cambridge University Press, Cambridge (2005)
21. Smith, E.E., Kosslyn, S.M.: Cognitive Psychology: Pearson New International Edition PDF eBook: Mind and Brain. Pearson Higher Education, London (2013)
22. Kumar, A., Irsoy, O., Ondruska, P., Iyyer, M., Bradbury, J., Gulrajani, I., Zhong, V., Paulus, R., Socher, R.: Ask me anything: dynamic memory networks for natural language processing. In: Proceedings of the International Conference on Machine Learning. The Proceedings of Machine Learning Research, pp. 1378–1387 (2016)
23. Xiong, C., Merity, S., Socher, R.: Dynamic memory networks for visual and textual question answering. In: Proceedings of the International Conference on Machine Learning. The Proceedings of Machine Learning Research, pp. 2397–2406 (2016)
24. Graves, A., Wayne, G., Danihelka, I.: Neural turing machines. arXiv:1410.5401 (2014)
25. Miller, A., Fisch, A., Dodge, J., Karimi, A.-H., Bordes, A., Weston, J.: Key-value memory networks for directly reading documents. arXiv:1606.03126 (2016)
26. Zhang, J., Shi, X., King, I., Yeung, D.-Y.: Dynamic key-value memory networks for knowledge tracing. In: Proceedings of the International Conference on World Wide Web, pp. 765–774 (2017)
27. Holyoak, K.J.: Analogy and relational reasoning. In: K. J. Holyoak & R. G. Morrison (Eds.), The Oxford handbook of thinking and reasoning, pp. 234–259. Oxford University Press, New York (2012)
28. Bahdanau, D., Cho, K., Bengio, Y.: Neural machine translation by jointly learning to align and translate. arXiv:1409.0473 (2014)
29. Xu, K., Ba, J., Kiros, R., Cho, K., Courville, A., Salakhudinov, R., Zemel, R., Bengio, Y.: Show, attend and tell: neural image caption generation with visual attention. In: Proceedings of the International Conference on Machine Learning. The Proceedings of Machine Learning Research, pp. 2048–2057 (2015)
30. Graves, A., Wayne, G., Reynolds, M., Harley, T., Danihelka, I. , Grabska-Barwińska, A., Colmenarejo, S.G., Grefenstette, E., Ramalho, T., Agapiou, J., et al.: Hybrid computing using a neural network with dynamic external memory. Nature **538**(7626), 471–476 (2016)
31. Raven, J.: Raven progressive matrices[M]. Springer, US (2003)
32. Carpenter, P.A., Just, M.A., Shell, P.: What one intelligence test measures: a theoretical account of the processing in the raven progressive matrices test. Psychol. Rev. **97**(3), 404 (1990)
33. Lovett, A., Tomai, E., Forbus, K., Usher, J.: Solving geometric analogy problems through two-stage analogical mapping. Cognit. Sci. **33**(7), 1192–1231 (2009)
34. Lovett, A., Forbus, K., Usher, J.: A structure-mapping model of raven's progressive matrices. In: Proceedings of the Annual Meeting of the Cognitive Science Society, vol. 32 (2010)
35. Zhang, C., Gao, F., Jia, B., Zhu, Y., Zhu, S.-C.: Raven: a dataset for relational and analogical visual reasoning. In: Proceedings of the IEEE/CVF Conference on Computer Vision and Pattern Recognition, pp. 5317–5327 (2019)
36. Hill, F., Santoro, A., Barrett, D.G., Morcos, A.S., Lillicrap, T.: Learning to make analogies by contrasting abstract relational structure. arXiv:1902.00120 (2019)
37. Steenbrugge, X., Leroux, S., Verbelen, T., Dhoedt, B.: Improving generalization for abstract reasoning tasks using disentangled feature representations. arXiv:1811.04784 (2018)
38. Van Steenkiste, S., Locatello, F., Schmidhuber, J., Bachem, O.: Are disentangled representations helpful for abstract visual reasoning? In: Proceedings of the Advances in Neural Information Processing Systems, vol. 32 (2019)

39. Zhuo, T., Kankanhalli, M.: Solving raven's progressive matrices with neural networks. arXiv:2002.01646 (2020)
40. Zheng, K., Zha, Z.-J., Wei, W.: Abstract reasoning with distracting features. In: Proceedings of the Advances in Neural Information Processing Systems, vol. 32 (2019)
41. Ichien, N., Liu, Q., Fu, S., Holyoak, K.J., Yuille, A., Lu, H.: Visual analogy: deep learning versus compositional models. arXiv:2105.07065 (2021)
42. Ronco, E., Gollee, H., Gawthrop, P.J.: Modular neural network and self-decomposition. Connect. Sci. (special issue: COMBINING NEURAL NETS) (1996)
43. Andreas, J., Rohrbach, M., Darrell, T., Klein, D.: Learning to compose neural networks for question answering. arXiv:1601.01705 (2016)
44. Hu, R., Rohrbach, M., Andreas, J., Darrell, T., Saenko, K.: Modeling relationships in referential expressions with compositional modular networks. In: Proceedings of the IEEE Conference on Computer Vision and Pattern Recognition, pp. 1115–1124 (2017)
45. Hu, R., Andreas, J., Rohrbach, M., Darrell, T., Saenko, K.: Learning to reason: end-to-end module networks for visual question answering. In: Proceedings of the IEEE International Conference on Computer Vision, pp. 804–813 (2017)
46. Hu, R., Andreas, J., Darrell, T., Saenko, K.: Explainable neural computation via stack neural module networks. In: Proceedings of the European Conference on Computer Vision, pp. 53–69 (2018)
47. Liu, D., Zhang, H., Wu, F., Zha, Z.-J.: Learning to assemble neural module tree networks for visual grounding. In: Proceedings of the IEEE/CVF International Conference on Computer Vision, pp. 4673–4682 (2019)
48. Kottur, S., Moura, J.M., Parikh, D., Batra, D., Rohrbach, M.: Visual coreference resolution in visual dialog using neural module networks. In: Proceedings of the European Conference on Computer Vision, pp. 153–169 (2018)
49. Jacobs, R.A., Jordan, M.I., Nowlan, S.J., Hinton, G.E.: Adaptive mixtures of local experts. Neural Comput. 3(1), 79–87 (1991)
50. Jordan, M.I., Jacobs, R.A.: Hierarchical mixtures of experts and the em algorithm. Neural Comput. 6(2), 181–214 (1994)
51. Riemer, M., Vempaty, A., Calmon, F., Heath, F., Hull, R., Khabiri, E.: Correcting forecasts with multifactor neural attention. In: Proceedings of the International Conference on Machine Learning. The Proceedings of Machine Learning Research, pp. 3010–3019 (2016)
52. Shazeer, N., Mirhoseini, A., Maziarz, K., Davis, A., Le, Q., Hinton, G., Dean, J.: Outrageously large neural networks: the sparsely-gated mixture-of-experts layer. arXiv:1701.06538 (2017)
53. Joulin, A., Mikolov, T.: Inferring algorithmic patterns with stack-augmented recurrent nets. In: Proceedings of the Advances in Neural Information Processing Systems, vol. 28 (2015)
54. Peng, H., Mou, L., Li, G., Liu, Y., Zhang, L., Jin, Z.: Building program vector representations for deep learning. In: Proceedings of the International Conference on Knowledge Science, Engineering and Management, pp. 547–553. Springer, Berlin (2015)
55. Zaremba, W., Sutskever, I.: Learning to execute. arXiv:1410.4615 (2014)
56. Lake, B.M., Salakhutdinov, R., Tenenbaum, J.B.: Human-level concept learning through probabilistic program induction. Science 350(6266), 1332–1338 (2015)
57. Li, C., Tarlow, D., Gaunt, A.L., Brockschmidt, M., Kushman, N.: Neural program lattices. In: International Conference on Learning Representations (2017)
58. Fox, R., Shin, R., Krishnan, S., Goldberg, K., Song, D., Stoica, I.: Parametrized hierarchical procedures for neural programming. In: Proceedings of the International Conference on Learning Representations (2018)
59. Johnson, J., Hariharan, B., Van Der Maaten, L., Hoffman, J., Fei-Fei, L., Lawrence Zitnick, C., Girshick, R.: Inferring and executing programs for visual reasoning. In: Proceedings of the IEEE International Conference on Computer Vision, pp. 2989–2998 (2017)
60. Chen, X., Liang, C., Yu, A.W., Zhou, D., Song, D., Le, Q.V.: Neural symbolic reader: scalable integration of distributed and symbolic representations for reading comprehension. In: Proceedings of the International Conference on Learning Representations (2019)

61. Vu, T., Haffari, G.: Automatic post-editing of machine translation: a neural programmer-interpreter approach. In: Proceedings of the Conference on Empirical Methods in Natural Language Processing, pp. 3048–3053 (2018)
62. Zellers, R., Bisk, Y., Farhadi, A., Choi, Y.: From recognition to cognition: visual commonsense reasoning. In: Proceedings of the IEEE/CVF Conference on Computer Vision and Pattern Recognition, pp. 6720–6731 (2019)
63. Chen, X., Jia, S., Xiang, Y.: A review: knowledge reasoning over knowledge graph. Exp. Syst. Appl. **141**, 112948 (2020)

Chapter 6
Decision-Based DCNs

Abstract This chapter first provides a brief overview of memory-based Deep Cognitive Networks (DCNs). Then, representative models from two aspects in terms of normative decision and descriptive decision are introduced and analyzed, as well as their relation to important theories, computational models and experimental evidences in cognitive psychology. At last, this chapter is briefly summarized.

Keywords Decision modeling. Group decision · Imitative reasoning

6.1 Overview

Decision is the process in which an agent chooses how to interact with external environment. It is very important for many real-world applications such as service robot and autonomous driving. As shown in Table 6.1, we mainly focus on two classes of decision-based DCNs: normative decision and descriptive decision, and their four sub-classes: sequential decision, group decision, emotional decision and imitative decision. The representative decision-based DCNs include Deep Q-Network [1, 2], Multi-agent Deep Reinforcement Learning [3, 4], Deep Counterfactual Regret Minimization [5, 6] and Deep Imitation Learning [7]. We also elaborate their related important theories, computational models and experimental evidences in cognitive psychology. The corresponding details will be explained in the following.

6.2 Normative Decision

In cognitive psychology, there are two major classes of decisions including normative decision and descriptive decision. The normative decision is related to normative theory or prescriptive theory for decision, which aims to tell an agent how to make ideal or rational decisions under given conditions [8]. The Expected Utility Theory (EUT) [9] is one of the most important theories in normative decision, which argues that actions should be selected according to the values of

Table 6.1 The taxonomy of decision-based DCNs

Class	Sub-class	Representative DCN	Theory, model and evidence
Normative decision	Sequential decision	Deep Q-network [1, 2], deep neural decision trees [20]	Expected utility theory [9], multi-attribute utility theory [10], normative model of decision making [25]
	Group decision	multi-agent deep reinforcement learning [3, 4]	
Descriptive decision	Emotional decision	Deep counterfactual regret minimization [5, 6]	Image theory [39, 40], bounded rationality theory [53], elimination by aspects [54]
	Imitative decision	Deep imitation learning [7], generative adversarial imitation learning [61]	

expected utilities. The higher the value is, the better the action is. Another important theory is the Multi-attribute Utility Theory (MUT) [10], which provides solutions to making more complex decisions by combining sub-decisions from different attribute dimensions. Next, we consider two sub-classes of normative decision in terms of sequential decision and group decision.

6.2.1 *Sequential Decision*

As shown in Fig. 6.1, Deep Q-Network (DQN) [1, 2] models the sequential decision as a Dynamic Markov Decision Process (DMDP) [11], which is able to predict an action to interact with external environment at each timestep. Coordinating with the main idea of EUT, each action is evaluated by a reward and the goal is to maximize aggregated rewards at all timesteps. The DQN was first proposed to address the major weakness of conventional RL, i.e., cannot well learn policies directly from high-dimensional data, which achieved human-level performance on a large set of Atari games.

Then, DQN has become a hot research topic and many researchers have proposed effective variants to address its limitations. Hasselt et al. [12] first found that the DQN sometimes substantially overestimates the values of actions, and then demonstrated that using the Double Q-Learning algorithm [13] can well alleviate this issue. Wang et al. [14] replaced conventional deep architectures such as CNNs with a new two-stream one, which can better suit for model-free RL. Considering that the DQN can only deal with discrete action spaces, Lillicrap et al. [15] combined deep learning and deterministic policy gradient algorithm [16]

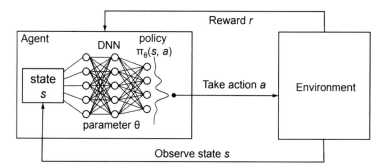

Fig. 6.1 Illustration of deep Q-network (DQN). At each timestep, an agent observes a state s and predicts an action a using a DNN. Based on the action, the state is updated and the agent receives a reward r. The parameter θ of DNN can be learnt by maximizing aggregated rewards at all timesteps. Figure is from [17]

together to better deal with physical control tasks having continuous (real-valued) action spaces. Up to now, various DQN-like models have been widely applied in many tasks that require for the interaction with environment including resource management [17], robot navigation [18], question answering [19] and game playing [1].

Note that there is another class of models that combines conventional Decision Tree (DT) and deep learning together as Deep Neural Decision Trees (DNDT) [20, 21] or Deep Neural Decision Forests (DNDF) [22, 23]. DNDT and DNDF can decompose given tasks into different sub-tasks, and then conquer them in a tree-structured manner. These models have been used in many supervised learning tasks such as image classification [24], semantic image labelling [22].

6.2.2 Group Decision

Different from previous sequential decision, group decision focuses on a set of agents rather than only one. Thus, the environment is more complex for each agent, since it is non-stationary and always dynamically affected by other agents. The relation among different agents is also diverse, which could be cooperative, competitive or even mixed. In cognitive psychology, the Normative Model of Decision Making (NMDM) [25] describes five different cases of group decision based on the degree of agent participation. As shown in Fig. 6.2, the Multi-agent Deep Reinforcement Learning (MDRL) [3, 4] is a commonly used approach for group decision, which can be roughly regarded as a multi-agent version of DQN. Similar to the five cases of NMDM, MDRL can also be further specified as different cases including Markov Game (MG) [26], Partially Observable Markov Game (POMG) [27] and Partially Observable Markov Decision Process (POMDP) [28], according to whether the environment state is fully and partially visible to agents.

Fig. 6.2 Illustration of
multi-agent deep
reinforcement learning
(MDRL). In this multi-agent
case, all agents jointly act on
the environment, and their
rewards depend on the result
of joint policy. Figure is from
[3]

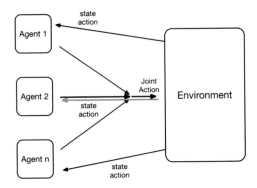

In particular, the MG includes a set of games that agents play repeatedly, in which the environment state summarizes the corresponding history of games. The representative applications are predator game [29] and iterated prisoner's dilemma [30]. Different from MG, the agents in POMG try to maximize their rewards in a partially observable environment. The representative applications are autonomous driving [31] and gridworld game [32]. Different from POMG that agents optimize individual rewards, the agents in POMDP usually optimize a joint reward. The representative applications are various real-time strategy games like Starcraft [33] and Dota2 [34]. There is another kind of setting named Extensive Form Game (EFM) [35], in which agents take actions sequentially. Such a sequential property is usually modeled as a game tree to show the order of actions in a long-term period. The well-known applications are games of poker [36] and go [37]. Note that there are also some works that do not use deep learning models, but still achieve very good performance on the game of poker [38].

6.3   Descriptive Decision

Different from normative decision, descriptive decision focuses on describing what humans actually make decisions in practice. For example, the Image Theory [39, 40] argues that humans in daily lives seldom make normative decisions. Instead, they just elaborate and evaluate the importance of all possible criteria, and then aggregate them to make the final decision. Next, we will analyze two sub-classes of descriptive decision in terms of emotional decision and imitative decision as follows.

6.3.1   Emotional Decision

It is widely recognized that humans usually cannot make fully rational decisions, since their emotions can greatly interfere the rational decision process [41, 42].

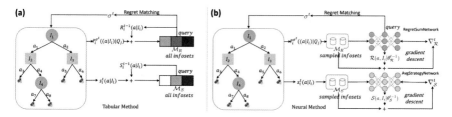

Fig. 6.3 Illustration of counterfactual regret minimization (CFR). Left (**a**): tabular based CFR uses two large tabular-based memories to store cumulative regrets. Right (**b**): neural network based CFR uses two DNNs to estimate cumulative regrets. Figure is from [6]

An early evidence is Allais paradox [43], which uncovers that the anticipated emotion of regret has clear impact on making decision. In addition, many emotional decision theories [44–46] all regard anticipated emotions, especially regret and disappointment, are crucial to the decision making in practice. These theories are not entirely opposed to the previous rational decision theories [9, 10], since these two kinds of theories are complementary and could be unified in the Dual System Theory [47].

However, in artificial intelligence, only a few works were proposed to model emotions during decision making. In 2007, Zinkevich et al. [48] proposed an early framework of Counterfactual Regret Minimization (CFR), as shown in Fig. 6.3. In the framework, regret value is defined as the difference between rewards of a candidate action and the action that has been actually taken. By minimizing cumulative regrets throughout the decision process, CFR is very useful for solving incomplete information games. Usually, regret matching [49] is an effective algorithm that is used by CFR for regret minimization due to its simplicity. There is a research direction of improving the efficiency of CFR, such as CFR+ [50] and Linear CFR [51], which achieve well performance on the game of poker.

However, these methods need to use large tabular-based memories to record cumulative regrets, which makes them cannot be easily applied to practical scenarios requiring high efficiency [52]. Recently, there are also some works trying to combine deep learning with CFR, such as using DNNs to approximate the behavior of conventional tabular in CFR in both single-agent setting [5] and multi-agent setting [6]. However, the total number of related works is still very small, and there is almost no work modeling other kinds of emotions.

6.3.2   Imitative Decision

In cognitive psychology, there are many important theories that are related to the descriptive decision. In 1955, Herbert Simon [53] proposed the Bounded Rationality Theory, which argues that an individual only has to find a satisfactory solution rather than the optimal one. In 1970, another theory called Elimination by Aspects

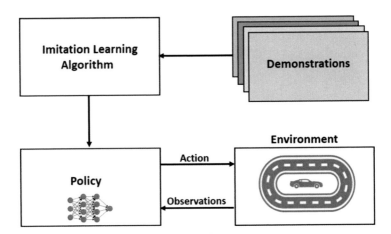

Fig. 6.4 Illustration of deep imitation learning (DIL). By imitating given demonstrations of several experts, an agent observes the environment and generates the policy to take actions based on deep learning models. Figure is from [69]

is proposed [54], which treats the process of decision making as performing a series of eliminations. In each elimination, an individual selects an attribute, and then eliminates some choices lacking that attribute. There are also some Other representative theories such as Prospect Theory [55] and Support Theory [56].

Although there are many related theories, only a few decision-based DCNs are proposed. Considering that directly modeling these theories is difficult, Deep Imitation Learning (DIL) [57] was proposed to implicitly encourage agents to imitate human experts' decisions based on deep learning models,[1] as shown in Fig. 6.4. There are two major types of DIL models: behavioural cloning and adversarial imitation learning. The first one [7, 59] tries to minimize the policy divergence between agents and experts, by reformulating the imitation learning to common classification tasks. In this direction, Pomerleau [60] proposed a very early behavioural cloning framework based on DNNs for the task of autonomous driving. The second one [61, 62] tries to maximize adversarial rewards of agents and experts, usually based on the inverse RL [63]. In this direction, Ho and Ermon proposed the most influential work [61] called Generative Adversarial Imitation Learning (GAIL), which generalizes the idea of discriminator [64] to distinguish polices made by agents and experts. In addition to robot navigation and manipulation [7, 65, 66], DIL has been applied to other tasks such as text classification [67] and chemical-graph generation [68].

---

[1] Note that the imitation learning is not new, which has been previously demonstrated to be effective in the field of robotics, also named as learning from demonstration [58].

6.4 Brief Summary

Currently, many important decision-based DCNs have been proposed for the sequential decision and group decision, which were successfully applied to the well-know tasks such as go and poker. But compared with existing works for normative decision, there are much fewer works modeling the descriptive decision. In fact, simulating human-like decision making process is under great demand in many practical scenarios such as autonomous driving and service robot.

References

1. Mnih, V., Kavukcuoglu, K., Silver, D., Graves, A., Antonoglou, I., Wierstra, D., Riedmiller, M.: Playing atari with deep reinforcement learning. arXiv:1312.5602 (2013)
2. Mnih, V., Kavukcuoglu, K., Silver, D., Rusu, A.A., Veness, J., Bellemare, M.G., Graves, A., Riedmiller, M., Fidjeland, A.K., Ostrovski, G., et al.: Human-level control through deep reinforcement learning. Nature **518**(7540), 529–533 (2015)
3. Du, W., Ding, S.: A survey on multi-agent deep reinforcement learning: from the perspective of challenges and applications. Artif. Intell. Rev. **54**(5), 3215–3238 (2021)
4. Wong, A., Bäck, T., Kononova, A.V., Plaat, A.: Multiagent deep reinforcement learning: challenges and directions towards human-like approaches. arXiv:2106.15691 (2021)
5. Jin, P., Keutzer, K., Levine, S.: Regret minimization for partially observable deep reinforcement learning. In: Proceedings of the International Conference on Machine Learning. The Proceedings of Machine Learning Research, pp. 2342–2351 (2018)
6. Li, H., Hu, K., Ge, Z., Jiang, T., Qi, Y., Song, L.: Double neural counterfactual regret minimization. arXiv:1812.10607 (2018)
7. Zhang, T., McCarthy, Z., Jow, O., Lee, D., Chen, X., Goldberg, K., Abbeel, P.: Deep imitation learning for complex manipulation tasks from virtual reality teleoperation. In: Proceedings of the IEEE International Conference on Robotics and Automation, pp. 5628–5635. IEEE, Piscataway (2018)
8. Edwards, W.: The theory of decision making. Psychol. Bullet. **51**(4), 380 (1954)
9. Schoemaker, P.J.: The expected utility model: its variants, purposes, evidence and limitations. J. Econ. Literature **20**, 529–563 (1982)
10. Winterfeldt, D.V., Fischer, G.W.: Multi-attribute utility theory: models and assessment procedures. Utility Probab. Hum. Decis. Making **11**, 47–85 (1975)
11. Puterman, M.L.: Markov decision processes. Handbooks Oper. Res. Manage. Sci. **2**, 331–434 (1990)
12. Van Hasselt, H., Guez, A., Silver, D.: Deep reinforcement learning with double q-learning. In: Proceedings of the AAAI Conference on Artificial Intelligence, vol. 30 (2016)
13. Hasselt, H.: Double q-learning. In: Proceedings of the Advances in Neural Information Processing Systems, vol. 23 (2010)
14. Wang, Z., Schaul, T., Hessel, M., Hasselt, H., Lanctot, M., Freitas, N.: Dueling network architectures for deep reinforcement learning. In: Proceedings of the International Conference on Machine Learning. The Proceedings of Machine Learning Research, pp. 1995–2003 (2016)
15. Lillicrap, T.P., Hunt, J.J., Pritzel, A., Heess, N., Erez, T., Tassa, Y., Silver, D., Wierstra, D.: Continuous control with deep reinforcement learning. arXiv:1509.02971 (2015)
16. Silver, D., Lever, G., Heess, N., Degris, T., Wierstra, D., Riedmiller, M.: Deterministic policy gradient algorithms. In: Proceedings of the International Conference on Machine Learning. The Proceedings of Machine Learning Research, pp. 387–395 (2014)

17. Mao, H., Alizadeh, M., Menache, I., Kandula, S.: Resource management with deep reinforcement learning. In: Proceedings of the ACM Workshop on Hot Topics in Networks, pp. 50–56 (2016)
18. Zhu, Y., Mottaghi, R., Kolve, E., Lim, J.J., Gupta, A., Fei-Fei, L., Farhadi, A.: Target-driven visual navigation in indoor scenes using deep reinforcement learning. In: Proceedings of the IEEE international Conference on Robotics and Automation, pp. 3357–3364. IEEE, Piscataway (2017)
19. Shen, Y., Huang, P.-S., Gao, J., Chen, W.: Reasonet: learning to stop reading in machine comprehension. In: Proceedings of the ACM SIGKDD International Conference on Knowledge Discovery and Data Mining, pp. 1047–1055 (2017)
20. Balestriero, R.: Neural decision trees. arXiv:1702.07360 (2017)
21. Yang, Y., Morillo, I.G., Hospedales, T.M.: Deep neural decision trees. arXiv:1806.06988 (2018)
22. Rota Bulo, S., Kontschieder, P.: Neural decision forests for semantic image labelling. In: Proceedings of the IEEE Conference on Computer Vision and Pattern Recognition, pp. 81–88 (2014)
23. Kontschieder, P., Fiterau, M., Criminisi, A., Bulom S.R.: Deep neural decision forests. In: Proceedings of the IEEE International Conference on Computer Vision, pp. 1467–1475 (2015)
24. Xiao, H.: NDT: neual decision tree towards fully functioned neural graph. arXiv:1712.05934 (2017)
25. Vroom, V.H., Yetton, P.W.: Leadership and Decision-Making, vol. 110. University of Pittsburgh, Pittsburgh (1973)
26. Littman, M.L.: Markov games as a framework for multi-agent reinforcement learning. In: Machine Learning Proceedings, pp. 157–163. Elsevier, Amsterdam (1994)
27. Hansen, E.A., Bernstein, D.S., Zilberstein, S.: Dynamic programming for partially observable stochastic games. In: Proceedings of the AAAI Conference on Artificial Intelligence, vol. 4, pp. 709–715 (2004)
28. Bernstein, D.S., Givan, R., Immerman, N., Zilberstein, S.: The complexity of decentralized control of Markov decision processes. Math. Oper. Res. **27**(4), 819–840 (2002)
29. Zheng, Y., Meng, Z., Hao, J., Zhang, Z.: Weighted double deep multiagent reinforcement learning in stochastic cooperative environments. In: Proceedings of the Pacific Rim International Conference on Artificial Intelligence, pp. 421–429. Springer, Berlin (2018)
30. Foerster, J.N., Chen, R.Y., Al-Shedivat, M., Whiteson, S., Abbeel, P., Mordatch, I. : Learning with opponent-learning awareness. arXiv:1709.04326 (2017)
31. Palanisamy, P.: Multi-agent connected autonomous driving using deep reinforcement learning. In: Proceedings of the International Joint Conference on Neural Networks, pp. 1–7. IEEE, Piscataway (2020)
32. Moreno, P., Hughes, E., McKee, K.R., Pires, B.A., Weber, T.: Neural recursive belief states in multi-agent reinforcement learning. arXiv:2102.02274 (2021)
33. Du, Y., Han, L., Fang, M., Liu, J., Dai, T., Tao, D.: LIIR: learning individual intrinsic reward in multi-agent reinforcement learning. In: Proceedings of the Advances in Neural Information Processing Systems, vol. 32 (2019)
34. Berner, C., Brockman, G., Chan, B., Cheung, V., Dębiak, P., Dennison, C., Farhi, D., Fischer, Q., Hashme, S., Hesse, C., et al.: Dota 2 with large scale deep reinforcement learning. arXiv:1912.06680 (2019)
35. Kuhn, H.W., Tucker, A.W.: Contributions to the Theory of Games, vol. 28. Princeton University Press, Princeton (1953)
36. Heinrich, J., Lanctot, M., Silver, D.: Fictitious self-play in extensive-form games. In: Proceedings of the International Conference on Machine Learning. The Proceedings of Machine Learning Research, pp. 805–813 (2015)
37. Silver, D., Huang, A., Maddison, C.J., Guez, A., Sifre, L., Van Den Driessche, G., Schrittwieser, J., Antonoglou, I., Panneershelvam, V., Lanctot, M., et al.: Mastering the game of go with deep neural networks and tree search. Nature **529**(7587), 484–489 (2016)

38. Brown, N., Sandholm, T.: Superhuman ai for heads-up no-limit poker: libratus beats top professionals. Science **359**(6374), 418–424 (2018)
39. Beach, L.R., Mitchell, T.R.: Image theory: principles, goals, and plans in decision making. Acta Psychol. **66**(3), 201–220 (1987)
40. Beach, L.R.: Image theory: personal and organizational decisions. In: Decision Making in Action: Models and Methods, pp. 148–157 (1993)
41. De Sousa, R.: The rationality of emotions. Dial. Can. Philos. Rev. **18**(1), 41–63 (1979)
42. Frank, R.H.: Passions Within Reason: The Strategic Role of the Emotions. WW Norton, New York (1988)
43. Allais, M.: Le comportement de l'homme rationnel devant le risque: critique des postulats et axiomes de l'école américaine. Econ. J. Econ. Soc. 503–546 (1953)
44. Mellers, B.A.: Choice and the relative pleasure of consequences. Psychol. Bullet. **126**(6), 910 (2000)
45. Bell, D.E.: Regret in decision making under uncertainty. Oper. Res. **30**(5), 961–981 (1982)
46. Bell, D.E.: Disappointment in decision making under uncertainty. Oper. Res. **33**(1), 1–27 (1985)
47. McClure, S.M., Laibson, D.I., Loewenstein, G., Cohen, J.D.: Separate neural systems value immediate and delayed monetary rewards. Science **306**(5695), 503–507 (2004)
48. Zinkevich, M., Johanson, M., Bowling, M., Piccione, C.: Regret minimization in games with incomplete information. In: Proceedings of the Advances in Neural Information Processing Systems, vol. 20 (2007)
49. Hart, S., Mas-Colell, A.: A simple adaptive procedure leading to correlated equilibrium. Econometrica **68**(5), 1127–1150 (2000)
50. Tammelin, O., Burch, N., Johanson, M., Bowling, M.: Solving heads-up limit texas hold'em. In: Proceedings of the International Joint Conference on Artificial Intelligence (2015)
51. Brown, N., Sandholm, N.: Solving imperfect-information games via discounted regret minimization. In: Proceedings of the AAAI Conference on Artificial Intelligence, vol. 33, pp. 1829–1836 (2019)
52. Burch, N.: Time and space: why imperfect information games are hard. PhD Thesis (2018)
53. Simon, H.A.: A behavioral model of rational choice. Quart. J. Econ. **69**(1), 99–118 (1955)
54. Tversky, A.: Elimination by aspects: a theory of choice. Psychol. Rev. **79**(4), 281 (1972)
55. Tversky, A., Kahneman, D.: Advances in prospect theory: cumulative representation of uncertainty. J. Risk Uncertain. **5**(4), 297–323 (1992)
56. Tversky, A., Koehler, D.J.: Support theory: a nonextensional representation of subjective probability. Psychol. Rev. **101**(4), 547 (1994)
57. Arulkumaran, K., Lillrank, D.O.: A pragmatic look at deep imitation learning. arXiv:2108.01867 (2021)
58. Argall, B.D., Chernova, S., Veloso, M., Browning, B.: A survey of robot learning from demonstration. Robot. Auton. Syst. **57**(5), 469–483 (2009)
59. Bain, M., Sammut, C.: A framework for behavioural cloning. In: Machine Intelligence, pp. 103–129 (1995)
60. Pomerleau, D.A.: ALVINN: an autonomous land vehicle in a neural network. In: Proceedings of the Advances in Neural Information Processing Systems, vol.1 (1988)
61. Ho, J., Ermon, S.: Generative adversarial imitation learning. In: Proceedings of the Advances in Neural Information Processing Systems, vol. 29 (2016)
62. Orsini, M., Raichuk, A., Hussenot, L., Vincent, D., Dadashi, R., Girgin, S., Geist, M., Bachem, O., Pietquin, O., Andrychowicz, M.: What matters for adversarial imitation learning? In: Proceedings of the Advances in Neural Information Processing Systems, vol. 34, pp. 14656–14668 (2021)
63. Ng, A.Y., Russell, S., et al.: Algorithms for inverse reinforcement learning. In: Proceedings of the International Conference on Machine Learning, vol. 1, p. 2 (2000)
64. Goodfellow, I., Pouget-Abadie, J., Mirza, M., Xu, B., Warde-Farley, D., Ozair, S., Courville, A., Bengio, Y.: Generative adversarial nets. In: Proceedings of the Advances in Neural Information Processing Systems, vol. 27 (2014)

65. Xu, D., Nair, S., Zhu, Y., Gao, J., Garg, A., Fei-Fei, L., Savarese, S.: Neural task programming: learning to generalize across hierarchical tasks. In: Proceedings of the IEEE International Conference on Robotics and Automation, pp. 3795–3802. IEEE, Piscataway (2018)
66. Wang, X., Huang, Q., Celikyilmaz, A., Gao, J., Shen, D., Wang, Y.-F., Wang, W.Y., Zhang, L.: Reinforced cross-modal matching and self-supervised imitation learning for vision-language navigation. In: Proceedings of the IEEE/CVF Conference on Computer Vision and Pattern Recognition, pp. 6629–6638 (2019)
67. Liu, M., Buntine, W., Haffari, G.: Learning how to actively learn: a deep imitation learning approach. In: Proceedings of the Annual Meeting of the Association for Computational Linguistics, pp. 1874–1883 (2018)
68. Jonas, E.: Deep imitation learning for molecular inverse problems. In: Proceedings of the Advances in Neural Information Processing Systems, vol. 32 (2019)
69. Kebria, P.M., Alizadehsani, R., Salaken, S.M., Hossain, I., Khosravi, A., Kabir, D., Koohestani, A., Asadi, H., Nahavandi, S., Tunsel, E., et al.: Evaluating architecture impacts on deep imitation learning performance for autonomous driving. In: Proceedings of the IEEE International Conference on Industrial Technology, pp. 865–870. IEEE, Piscataway (2019)

Chapter 7
Conclusions and Future Trends

Abstract This chapter first provides conclusions of the whole book, by summarizing major properties of different Deep Cognitive Networks (DCNs). Afterwards, we discuss some open problems for future research directions.

Keywords Model interpretability · Computational cost · Comprehensive modeling

7.1 Conclusions

In this book, we have introduced various DCNs and analyzed their relation to important theories, computational models and experimental evidences in cognitive psychology. All the DCNs are categorized into four classes including attention-based DCNs, memory-based DCNs, reasoning-based DCNs and decision-based DCNs, according to their modeled cognitive mechanisms. The major conclusions are summarized as follows.

1. **Attention-based DCNs.** The major advantage of attention-based DCNs is that they can selectively extract salient information from redundant background. This property enables attention-based DCNs to achieve better performance in information extraction tasks such as image captioning [1] and machine translation [2]. Hard attention and soft attention are two major classes of attention-based DCNs. Compared with hard attention, soft attention has been used more widely and shown better performance in a wide range of applications. Self attention is a sub-class of soft attention, which plays an essential role in Transformer [3], as well as various pretrained models such as BERT [4] and ViT [5].
2. **Memory-based DCNs**: The major advantage of memory-based DCNs is that they can store historical information in an external memory module, which can be later reused for reference. This property enables memory-based DCNs to better deal with the problems of few-shot learning [6] and long-range dependency modeling [7]. Short-term memory and long-term memory are two major types of memory-based DCNs. Either short-term memory or long-term

© The Author(s), under exclusive license to Springer Nature Singapore Pte Ltd. 2023   59
Y. Huang, L. Wang, *Deep Cognitive Networks*, SpringerBriefs in Computer Science,
https://doi.org/10.1007/978-981-99-0279-8_7

memory has drawn much attention, and many related memory-based DCNs have been proposed. Among them, Memory Network [8] and its extensions [9, 10] are the most widely studied models, which are demonstrated to be very useful especially for the task of question answering.

3. **Reasoning-based DCNs**: The major advantage of reasoning-based DCNs is that they can infer desired conclusions by analyzing the relation among given premises. This property enables reasoning-based DCNs to better handle semantic reasoning tasks such as IQ test [11] and puzzle solving [12]. Analogical reasoning and deductive reasoning are two major types of reasoning-based DCNs. Among them, only a few reasoning-based DCNs [13, 14] are proposed to model the compositional reasoning and programmed reasoning. However, their results are very interesting and promising, which demonstrate that DCNs are able to achieve human-like performance of cognitive reasoning.

4. **Decision-based DCNs**: The major advantage of decision-based DCNs is that they can dynamically interact with external environment. This property is very useful for service robot and autonomous driving to make suitable decisions in real-world scenarios. Normative decision and descriptive decision are two major types of decision-based DCNs. Compared with descriptive decision, there are much more decision-DCNs are proposed to model the normative decision. Among them, the most successful ones are Deep Q-Network [15, 16] and its multi-agent versions [17], whose effectiveness has been demonstrated in many well-known applications such as go [18].

7.2   Open Problems and Future Trends

Based on what we have analyzed, we find that there are still a number of open problems in terms of comprehensive modeling, model interpretability, evaluation scenario and computational cost, which are briefly discussed as follows.

1. **Comprehensive Modeling**. Currently, the modeling of attention is extensively studied, while there still needs more research for the modeling of other mechanisms. For example, the explicit memory has been mostly considered, while the implicit memory is seldom studied. And, how to better model the semantic memory with dynamic evens remains to be a great challenge. In addition to the already mentioned attention, memory, reasoning and decision, there are more other kinds of cognitive mechanisms or processes in human brains. How to well model them and let them corporate to achieve stronger cognitive abilities is another challenge.

2. **Model Interpretability**. The DCNs stand at the cutting edge of disciplines of artificial intelligence and cognitive psychology. We just coarsely connect existing DCNs with important theories, computational models and experimental evidences in cognitive psychology. So it would be better that more researchers from different disciplines work together to further improve the model interpretability of DCNs, as well as propose new and biologically plausible DCNs. In fact, the

achieved progress in DCNs might also inspire cognitive psychologists to better understand cognitive mechanisms in their research.

3. **Evaluation Scenario**. Currently, the performance of most DCNs is evaluated only by the model accuracy on publicly available datasets. Compared with conventional deep learning models, the advantages of DCNs lie in their cognitive abilities such as selective information extraction, knowledge reuse and dynamic reasoning, which are very useful for dealing with spatial-temporal redundant information and few/zero-shot content in dynamical open-set practical scenarios. Therefore, more suitable evaluation datasets and scenarios for DCNs are under great demand.

4. **Computational Cost**. Human brains can process their perceived information efficiently, while current DCNs based on deep learning usually have very large numbers of parameters. Their computational cost is usually very high especially when processing large-scale data. Therefore, studying more efficient DCNs is very important for practical use. In the future, the computational cost of DCNs could be reduced by: (1) using more efficient deep learning models as backbones, and (2) modeling new cognitive mechanisms accounting for the efficiency in human brains.

References

1. Xu, K., Ba, J., Kiros, R., Cho, K., Courville, A., Salakhudinov, R., Zemel, R., Bengio, Y.: Show, attend and tell: neural image caption generation with visual attention. In: Proceedings of the International Conference on Machine Learning, pp. 2048–2057 (2015)
2. Bahdanau, D., Cho, K., Bengio, Y.: Neural machine translation by jointly learning to align and translate. arXiv:1409.0473 (2014)
3. Vaswani, A., Shazeer, N., Parmar, N., Uszkoreit, J., Jones, L., Gomez, A.N., Kaiser, Ł., Polosukhin, I.: Attention is all you need. In: Proceedings of the Advances in Neural Information Processing Systems, vol. 30 (2017)
4. Devlin, J., Chang, M.-W., Lee, K., Toutanova, K.: Bert: pre-training of deep bidirectional transformers for language understanding. arXiv:1810.04805 (2018)
5. Dosovitskiy, A., Beyer, L., Kolesnikov, A., Weissenborn, D., Zhai, X., Unterthiner, T., Dehghani, M., Minderer, M., Heigold, G., Gelly, S., et al.: An image is worth 16x16 words: transformers for image recognition at scale. arXiv:2010.11929 (2020)
6. Santoro, A., Bartunov, S., Botvinick, M., Wierstra, D., Lillicrap, T.: Meta-learning with memory-augmented neural networks. In: Proceedings of the International Conference on Machine Learning. The Proceedings of Machine Learning Research, pp. 1842–1850 (2016)
7. Wang, J., Wang, W., Huang, Y., Wang, L., Tan, T.: M3: multimodal memory modelling for video captioning. In: Proceedings of the IEEE Conference on Computer Vision and Pattern Recognition, pp. 7512–7520 (2018)
8. Weston, J., Chopra, S., Bordes, A.: Memory networks. arXiv:1410.3916 (2014)
9. Sukhbaatar, S., Weston, J., Fergus, R., et al.: End-to-end memory networks. In: Proceedings of the Advances in Neural Information Processing Systems, vol. 28 (2015)
10. Kumar, A., Irsoy, O., Ondruska, P., Iyyer, M., Bradbury, J., Gulrajani, I., Zhong, V., Paulus, R., Socher, R.: Ask me anything: dynamic memory networks for natural language processing. In: Proceedings of the International Conference on Machine Learning. The Proceedings of Machine Learning Research, pp. 1378–1387 (2016)

11. Hoshen, D., Werman, M.:IQ of neural networks. arXiv:1710.01692 (2017)
12. Pierrot, T., Ligner, G., Reed, S.E., Sigaud, O., Perrin, N., Laterre, A., Kas, D., Beguir, K., de Freitas, N.: Learning compositional neural programs with recursive tree search and planning. In: Proceedings of the Advances in Neural Information Processing Systems, vol. 32 (2019)
13. Andreas, J., Rohrbach, M., Darrell, T., Klein, D.: Neural module networks. In: Proceedings of the IEEE Conference on Computer Vision and Pattern Recognition, pp. 39–48 (2016)
14. Neelakantan, A., Le, Q.V., Sutskever, I.: Neural programmer: inducing latent programs with gradient descent. arXiv:1511.04834 (2015)
15. Mnih, V., Kavukcuoglu, K., Silver, D., Graves, A., Antonoglou, I., Wierstra, D., Riedmiller, M.: Playing atari with deep reinforcement learning. arXiv:1312.5602 (2013)
16. Mnih, V., Kavukcuoglu, K., Silver, D., Rusu, A.A., Veness, J., Bellemare, M.G., Graves, A., Riedmiller, M., Fidjeland, A.K., Ostrovski, G., et al.: Human-level control through deep reinforcement learning. Nature **518**(7540), 529–533 (2015)
17. Du, W., Ding, S.: A survey on multi-agent deep reinforcement learning: from the perspective of challenges and applications. Artif. Intell. Rev. **54**(5), 3215–3238 (2021)
18. Silver, D., Huang, A., Maddison, C.J., Guez, A., Sifre, L., Van Den Driessche, G., Schrittwieser, J., Antonoglou, I., Panneershelvam, V., Lanctot, M., et al.: Mastering the game of go with deep neural networks and tree search. Nature **529**(7587), 484–489 (2016)

Printed in the United States
by Baker & Taylor Publisher Services